STOP PUTTING OUT FIRES

BUILDING A MORE EFFICIENT AND PROFITABLE LAW PRACTICE

JEREMY W. RICHTER

scarlet oak press

ISBN: 978-1-7336655-0-6

Library of Congress Control Number: 2019902029

Cover design by Cary Chu

www.carychu.com

Published by Scarlet Oak Press

www.scarletoakpress.com

Printed in the United States of America

For Anna, Jack, and Caroline, who provide me with the motivation and inspiration to do my best work.

PRAISE FOR STOP PUTTING OUT FIRES

With a friendly but authoritative voice, Richter shares telling anecdotes and practical insights aimed at helping young lawyers hit the ground running.

— ROSS GUBERMAN, AUTHOR OF *POINT MADE* AND CREATOR OF BRIEFCATCH

Stop Putting Out Fires is a must-read for any lawyer who wants to thrive — and not just survive — in the practice of law. Though entertaining examples make his points, Richter's advice resonates in stark reality.

— ANNE BLUME, CEO OF CLAIMS AND LITIGATION MANAGEMENT ALLIANCE

Once again, Jeremy has put together a readable and practical guide for developing your law practice. Told through a series of vignettes, this easy to read book will set you on the path to master your schedule, improve your practice, and hopefully be a happier lawyer.

— KEITH LEE, FOUNDER OF LAWYERSMACK AND ASSOCIATE'S MIND

Stop Putting Out Fires is described by the author Jeremy Richter--a Birmingham, Alabama litigator--as a "devotional for lawyers." This wonderful, practical book is written in engaging, accessible prose. You can start with any chapter, any story. It's well designed for the busy junior lawyer looking for ideas on how to improve how they manage cases and how they work with clients. *Stop Putting Out Fires* covers an impressive range of topics, from what partners expect of associates to the myth that law firm marketing is only for extroverts to building an effective law firm website. A strength of this book is Richter's storytelling. *Stop Putting Out Fires* is filled with entertaining anecdotes from the author's life and law practice. With *Stop Putting Out Fires*, Richter has gifted the lawyer community with important lessons packaged in a delightful, user-friendly format.

— Katrina Lee, Author of *The Legal Career: Knowing the Business, Thriving in Practice*

CONTENTS

INTRODUCTION

Stop putting out fires! Or at least, stop *just* putting out fires. There are days you wake up knowing what you need to accomplish. But by the time you walk into the office, you've begun to be inundated with emails, your voicemail light is blinking, and there is a stack of documents that came in the mail and have been placed in your chair. You allow your plans to go out the window, tending now to what seems urgent rather than the work that is important.

When you are disorganized and popping from one urgent task to another, trying to put out fires that are cropping up all over your practice, you are not being the best lawyer or business person you can be. I want to help you change that.

Putting out fires is a reactionary tactic. It is what you have to do when you are disorganized and haven't put preventive measures in place. And who knows what is hiding in the undergrowth and deadfall you've allowed to pile up? Kindling just waiting to turn into a raging wildfire with the smallest ember. Sometimes that comes in the form of demanding clients and others as unwieldy cases.

Nothing will derail plans you have for your day faster than

a client calling with what they claim is an emergency. And they probably believe it is an emergency. But if your experience has taught you anything, it is that there are few emergencies in the law. Even so, your client demands your attention and your time.

If you allow them to disrupt your day, you will have gone from knowing exactly what you will do today to now having a morning meeting that will last much longer than it should. Your trial brief that is due will be postponed and your inbox will continue to grow with unread messages. Your productive plans will have gone up in smoke.

But since you can't have a law practice without clients, you might as well learn to deal with them. And sometimes that means putting needy clients on ice for a bit. A plaintiff's lawyer told me a story that she once had a client call her at 8:00pm on Christmas Eve. She hadn't recognized the number and answered anyway with tape on her fingers as she wrapped Christmas presents. The client identified himself.

The lawyer replied, "If this isn't an emergency, it needs to wait."

Her client decried, "It is! It's an emergency."

She could feel the trap door, but took another step anyway, "Okay. What is it?"

"What's the status of my case?" His case was a car wreck suit that had been filed recently.

She felt her blood pressure rising and responded, "Listen. If you need a lawyer who's available on Christmas Eve to talk with you about your case, you need to find a new one. I'm not your girl."

With this book, I want to share with you ideas for managing your clients, cases, and practice in more effective ways. To help you put systems in place so you can be prepared for when something unexpected happens. Being organized and having systematic approaches to client communication and case management enables you to be positioned to act with a measured response and allocate resources as needed. That's what this book is intended to help you do. *Stop Putting Out Fires* addresses the aspects of your work as a lawyer that you interact with on a daily (even hourly) basis.

I will provide you with tools to better manage your cases, clients, practice, and even other lawyers in your firm. Employing the tools, methods, and systems you read about will enable you to be more efficient, more effective, and as a result, more profitable.

Think of this book as a devotional for lawyers. Spend a few minutes each weekday for the next nine weeks reading a chapter from this book and you will walk away with practical ideas to improve the ways you handle cases, relate to clients, and manage your practice. My objective for *Stop Putting Out Fires* is that I will provide you with ideas that will enable you to have happier clients, get better results, and make more money.

PART I

CLIENT MANAGEMENT

1

SURVIVAL OF THE MOST ADAPTABLE

O nce upon a time and persisting for many years, when I was awakened in the night or early morning, I found it difficult to go back to sleep. Whatever the reason for being awakened. No matter how tired I was. I just had a hard time going back to sleep. I lay awake for long stretches trying to will myself back to sleep, which incidentally is more stress-inducing than relaxing.

Then I became a parent. You may know this already (and I was only recently reminded with the arrival of our second child), but newborns have to eat every couple of hours. Day and night. This means the baby's parents have to wake up every couple of hours to change wet/dirty diapers and feed her.

For me, of course, this was problematic. If I would be woken up every 2-3 hours, then remain awake for an interminable period after that, I would get little sleep. I had to adapt or be lost to some sleepless zombie-like existence. As it turns out, the human body is pretty adaptable in dire circumstances. I can now wake up, change a diaper, hand a kid off to her mommy for feeding, and go back to sleep (even with a lamp on). I know— it's amazing.

Being adaptable in your practice

Guess what? Both the legal and business side of being a lawyer demand malleability as well. Caselaw and statutes change. Clients' demands and the clients themselves change. Overhead costs and business expenses are never static for long. These things require you to be adaptable to maintain long-term success. Here are a couple of adaptations you can make to stay on top of things:

Be aware of your clients' needs. Anticipate your clients' needs and meet them in advance. This builds trust with your clients and keeps them satisfied. And don't forget that for all our high falutin' lawyerly ways, we are a service industry. In some ways, we are functionally no different from your mechanic or exterminator. When clients come to us with a problem, we need to be prepared to address that problem and think of things the client may not yet have considered.

This level of service and forethought will continue to build trusty equity with your clients and keep them happy with your work. Maintaining the client as the priority in your practice will keep you ahead of the field of lawyers who view clients and obstacles and impediments to be avoided. The trouble with that mindset is that without clients, we don't have a business to operate and don't get to practice anything.

Use technology to your advantage. Technology continues to evolve in ways that enable us to more efficiently represent our clients and handle their problems. Clients likewise can track case expenses and compare the costs they incur with us against that of other lawyers they use. It's becoming increasingly important that you manage your work in the most efficient manner possible.

"Business as usual" isn't the way forward

Don't be a victim of doing "business as usual." There's an episode of *The Office* where Ryan is implementing wholesale changes to the business model, and Michael Scott is having trouble with it.

Ryan: OK, what's up?

Michael: Yeah, 'kay. I was just... After the presentation, just wanted to make sure, that vis-a-vis, that everything in the office is business as usual?

Ryan: Well it is business, but not as usual.

Michael: Yeah, I know I understand... we're making great strides and we're updating, but business as usual, no?

Ryan: No. We're throwing out the entire playbook, we're starting from scratch, we're implementing a brand new system.

Michael: Good, so, we're on the same page?

Ryan: No. We're not. Michael, I know exactly how much time and man power are wasted in this branch. This company is getting younger, faster, more efficient. You need to prepare yourself.

The environment around you is evolving at a rapid pace. Many tools can make your practice and case management easier and more efficient. Tools that you can program to prompt you to undertake certain tasks. Things that will enable you to more easily keep abreast of your caseload. But if you're the curmudgeon who refuses to use email or otherwise update your practice, you're going to miss out on opportunities to serve your clients better. To keep up and effectively represent your clients, you need to be adaptable.

2

FAILURE TO COMMUNICATE CAN COST YOU CLIENTS

I n early March 2018, I flew from Birmingham to Minneapolis, where I rented a vehicle and drove to Wisconsin. The next day I drove back to Minneapolis and returned my rental car. I took the tram to the terminal where I got my ticket and went through security. As I was getting redressed after going through the TSA scanners and began rearranging my belongings, I realized I had left my sunglasses in the car. Looking at my watch and then at the security lines, I realized I didn't have time to go back to the car rental location, get my sunglasses, then go back through security.

I called the car rental company, went through about a dozen automated menus, and finally got through to the rental desk at Minneapolis-St. Paul airport, Terminal 1, where the phone rang and rang and rang and ... went to voicemail. I left a message explaining the situation — I had *just* left my sunglasses in my vehicle; if you call me back right away, you may be able to get them to me before my departure. I called seven more times after that, and no one ever answered the phone.

I called the next day, and no one answered the phone. No one ever called me back. Two days later, I saw on the rental company's lost-and-found page for Minneapolis-St. Paul airport, Terminal 1 that a pair of sunglasses had been found. I filled out report, submitted it, and waited. And waited. Six days, I waited. Nothing. So I went to Twitter to air my grievances.

The rental car company responded to my tweet and we had a good conversation by direct message, and they were reassuring. The next day, I got an email that my sunglasses had not been found. A couple of days after that, the rental company's Twitter guy sent me a message asking me to rate my experience.

The guy didn't know what he had asked for, because he got both barrels in the most polite-but-displeased manner available to me. I owned up to losing my sunglasses. That's on me. But then I called trying to get them to resolve a minor problem for me. Nine times, I called. I never got an answer. I had left a message right after the problem arose making them aware of the minor problem and asking for help in resolving it. Never did I receive any response. The Twitter guy reassured me that the rental company was doing everything in its power to locate my lost item and that he had asked someone from the location at Minneapolis-St. Paul airport to give me a call.

Several days later they did call and put me on hold for ten minutes while they searched lost-and-found. They reported back that they did not find my sunglasses. The 10-minute search did cause me to wonder how thorough a search had been performed when I got my first email notice. I was promised a phone call the next day. I did not expect to be called back, and I was not disappointed. But I did receive another email confirming my lost item had not been found.

What if I failed to communicate with my clients?

Let's apply this to a legal context with the following hypothetical: A current client calls me with a minor problem. I'm busy, so

I don't answer the phone. He leaves a message, telling me what his small problem is and that if I respond to his message promptly, I can probably solve his small problem quickly and keep it from escalating. But I don't return his call. It's not personal; it's just that I can't be bothered about it. Not only that, I ignore his next seven calls. I even refuse to answer the phone when he calls the next day. The day after that, he sends me an email, telling me his problem was worsened. Sorry, dude, I'm not going to reply. Got other stuff going on. But even if I didn't, I'm probably not going to reply.

Days later, he calls my boss telling him about the problem. My boss believes in me, so he reassures my client that I'm a good lawyer and an upstanding guy, and he's sure that I'm on top of it. But I'm not any of those things. The boss brings the call to my attention, so the next day, I fire off an email, "Sorry. Can't help."

More days go by, and my client calls my boss again. And despite all the mounting evidence to the contrary, my boss still believes that I'm not a scoundrel and assures the client that I will call him. Then the boss tells me to call the client. Do I call him? Nope. I don't call or respond in any way.

You know what happens next in this scenario? My client fires me. Rightfully. Not only is he going to fire me, he's never going to use me again. And he's going to do his darnedest to make sure no one he knows does either. He called me with a small problem, which was clearly his fault but which I could have easily solved for him. But I just ignored him altogether and with total indifference. Now his problem will cost him money out of his pocket that could have been avoided if I could have only been bothered to respond to him promptly.

When you choose not to communicate with your clients, what you are actually communicating to them is that they and their business are unimportant to you. I'm sure none of you would ignore your clients like that. But if you were otherwise inclined to, I would implore you not to do that. It's not nice (to put it mildly), and your (former) client might just put you on blast to everyone who reads his blog and follows him on social media. Or on your Google reviews. Or to the state bar.

You get the idea. Just communicate with your clients in a timely and effective manner. It's good for everyone.

3

HOW YOU CAN MAKE LIFE EASIER FOR YOUR CLIENTS

I f you can't keep your clients happy, you aren't going to keep your clients. When your clients are corporations that have lawyers handling their business all over the country, those clients know exactly what they want, and how and when they want it. You and I need to know those things as well, so we can be compliant and make their jobs easier.

Outside counsel have the difficult job of managing the litigation and other assignments from in-house counsel. And as important as getting good results is, communicating with in-house counsel is no less so. From where I sit, there are three general categories of communications that are important for outside counsel to maintain: (1) the value of early and accurate evaluations for both liability and monetary value of a claim, (2) the importance of accurate litigation budgets, and (3) the need for quality and timely reporting on case developments and compliance with guidelines.

But I didn't want to be presumptuous, so I reached out to some in-house lawyers to ask what was important to them. At first, I wasn't sure how willing they would be to share their responses with me, but I quickly received an encouraging general consensus: "I'm not sure I have ever passed up an opportunity to help outside counsel make my life easier. It's one of my favorite cycles of mutual benefit."

The in-house lawyers I spoke with work in a wide variety of sectors and provided some insightful answers that if implemented, can help outside counsel make the lives of in-house counsel easier and keep them happy so they'll keep sending us work.

The value of early and accurate evaluations of both liability and the monetary value of claims

Burt: Early and accurate assessments for any given problem are key to continuing to get asked the question / assigned the matter.

Jules: An early case assessment, which is accurate and provides the basis of the assumptions it makes, is very important. We will use that to come up with a risk-adjusted value of the matter. That risk-adjusted number is hopefully going to be directionally accurate due to the early case assessment and outside counsel's experience in the relevant jurisdiction. (We don't discount intuition/gut feel from experienced local counsel, but we do need to understand their experience level). That number will inform our resolution strategy and the level of attention we devote to the matter internally. We place an incredibly high value on opportunity costs, so knowing early what a reasonable settlement is adds a lot of value for us. We tend to involve litigators early on in potential disputes, in order to aim at an earlier resolution. We think it works.

Jenn: I think it's an interesting topic, because I am often very involved with issues that we know will result in litigation. So I may use outside counsel to help "gut check" my evaluation of liability or value of a claim, but I don't rely on them much for that. If they disagree with my analysis, I certainly want to know about that, but I haven't had that situation come up yet.

Connor: This is helpful but not as important with a lot of in-house litigation. In-house litigation isn't usually about damages recovery, it's about maintaining a market position. In other words, you might spend more on a case than you recover, but that is fine because you establish boundaries around your brand/position. Same thing with defending suits at trial vs settling - if a company is worried about setting a bad precedent, it makes sense to spend the money to try to defend. And although this isn't something you can't really talk about out loud, there is an aspect of "If I keep pushing this, I'll get them to go away as a nuisance cost," and that matters a lot.

The other piece is that a surprising amount of in-house litigation is ego driven, as in, someone founded a company, had moderate success, and has now tied their entire self-worth to it. Also, they are used to getting their way. So it's nothing for a CEO to say, "I don't care how much it costs – I want these guys stopped!"

This puts in-house counsel in a tough spot - how do you explain to the person that can fire you that the claim isn't worth it? It's helpful to have solid outside counsel that will support this with a solid valuation. But that valuation can't be, "Well, this is an average settlement versus this is an average trial cost." The better outside counsel understands my business and my market, the better they can advise on things like whether or not this has far reaching implications.

The importance of realistic litigation budgets

Connor: This is harder to predict in a helpful way, as it depends on the company. All companies do legal bills differently. I've been at some where the legal department had a litigation budget, I've been at some where it was a general expense. Plus a lot of companies have some insurance policies for that sort of thing. I've also never specifically had to make a case budget, so I don't have much experience. One thing I will say is that if you are going to add on fancy things (like a mock jury) you better be able to show a return on investment.

The other piece is to keep in mind that if you present a budget, in-house counsel will take that to the executive leadership and hopefully get approval. If outside counsel blows that budget, then in-house now has to go to their decision maker and present that. Basically, you are getting fired ASAP.

Jules: I don't place much importance on litigation budgets. I want something which is in the right ballpark and is directionally accurate so that the business isn't surprised. As an enterprise, we don't do much budgeting and don't see much value in it. Being privately held lets us focus on the long-term value. On any large matter, I will be looking for some type of fee agreement anyway. My current favorite version of those, which was suggested to me by outside counsel, is a flat fee (invoiced monthly) with a risk collar. Everyone has skin in the game that way and shares the same incentives.

The last matter I did this on, our risk-adjusted value was re-done three times as we headed to a final arbitration hearing. The legal fees stayed the same in each analysis because we discount sunk costs, and the counter-party did a number of things that made the matter more expensive. The key to this is that I (and subsequently the business) was not surprised. Outside counsel and I discussed strategies, and that discussion always included a note on whether it would be more expensive than we planned. On an original $1.5M fee estimate, the final cost was $2.3M. The relatively high percentage variance wasn't a problem because everyone was on the same page.

The need for quality and timely reporting on case developments and compliance with guidelines.

Connor: I'll tell you a story - we contracted a doc review firm to review about a million documents. I sat next to the project manager every day. We basically spoke throughout the day all day. He sent reports periodically, which I actually opened. Then, one day, my boss asked me to find out what the responsiveness rate was on the documents, so when I got to the review center I asked him. He gave a great answer, talked me through the numbers, what they meant, how they compared to expected, the whole nine. He even showed me a report that laid it out nicely. I said, "That's great. Can I get this to share with the team?" He politely told me that he sent it every night around 7:00pm in this nightly email.

The point is: I (and the team) expected nightly reports. If we didn't receive them, we would have noticed. But we also never read them, and when we needed an actual update, we expected someone to just give us the answer. But we also didn't want outside counsel to present it directly to management.

I guess the take-away is, have regular updates going out, but at the end of the day, the client is going to call you to talk through the details.

Jenn: Complying with engagement and invoicing guidelines is surprisingly key to me. I know they are a pain (and that ours in particular are a pain), but it builds so much trust. I don't want to have to review every invoice in mind-numbing detail. If you show me you are trustworthy on the smaller, less important things, it carries over to the big things.

With regard to litigation guidelines and updates, I will generally be very specific about what I want, and it will vary significantly by matter. I will clue you in on who is important internally, and if you want, I will get you on the phone with them and help solidify that relationship, but I never want to be surprised on that call. We should have already talked about it. Those updates, and the level of detail in them, can be critical to me internally and to getting appropriate authority for resolving the matter.

There are some matters that I will just expect updates and will let you run with. There are others that you will essentially have in-house counsel as full members of your team. The goal is for our team (in-house and outside counsel) to operate as smoothly as if we were one group. When it works, it is a beautiful thing with better resolutions. That is something that not all outside counsel are willing to engage in, and sometimes it's simply difficult with competing schedules, but I need to know up-front if the staffing or communication plan has you concerned.

Other Important Issues for In-House Counsel

Connor: I know multi-tasking is the way the world works, but every time we call counsel, if someone can hear typing in the background, someone immediately mutes the phone, rolls their eyes and says, "He is double billing." It's in-house's favorite game.

Also, don't underestimate the fact that outside counsel is the fall guy if management decides the case isn't going the way management would like. In-house will pay outside counsel's fees because it means in-house gets to blame outside counsel and keep their own job.

Jenn: The absolute most important thing that makes my life easier is early notice of deadlines where you need my help: gathering documents, arranging witness interviews, reviewing things that need my input, etc. The worst situation is when outside counsel comes to me with discovery responses that I need to review, find accurate factual information for, and find someone to verify them, all on the day they must be served. That happened to me recently, and it was a real last-minute scramble.

The best way to avoid it is early and frequent communication. Just because outside counsel sends me an email doesn't mean I'll act on it right away. I think this is true for most in-house counsel - I need follow up, or it will easily fall off my radar.

Suzie: It is important for outside counsel to provide "lessons learned." If something is broken, tell us what is broken that we need to fix. One of my biggest pet peeves was when I'd find out from outside counsel that we had the same exact issue or problem come up several times, yet here we are still litigating it. Outside counsel needs to communicate what went wrong so we have an opportunity to fix it.

Learn as much as you can about the business. We often had outside counsel want to settle employment cases with non-monetary relief, like training for a bunch of employees. At [Big Box Store], we needed everyone selling stuff out on the sales floor. Taking time to train people meant hours and hours of people not selling. Most of the time, we'd rather pay money to settle a case than have to train a bunch of people. You have to understand how a business works to know those kinds of things.

We had other quirks like that as well. We'd sometimes settle stuff for gift cards. It was way cheaper for us to pay out a gift card than cash. Then you had the added bonus that people would keep shopping at your store because they had a gift card rather than going to a competitor.

One of our goals as outside counsel is to make life easier for our clients by providing timely and effective communication. Sometimes that communication concerns the value of cases, budget changes, or developments in a case. But to best serve our clients, we need to know what they're looking for and how they want that information presented. If your client isn't forthcoming with this in the way of litigation guidelines or other reporting instructions, don't be afraid to ask. In the words of G. I. Joe, "Knowing is half the battle."

4

LITIGATION BUDGETS SHOULD REFLECT REALITY

L aw firms should base their case budgeting processes on real numbers that better enable clients to manage litigation costs and set reserves. Undoubtedly, litigation budgets can change during the course of litigation, but attorneys need to notify their clients as soon as practicable of expected upticks in case expenses that require budget increases.

Too often, when preparing litigation budgets for clients, lawyers copy-and-paste a set of numbers from one report to the next without stopping to consider the fees and expenses that may be linked to individual cases. Like many things, budgets require some experience to do well, but they also require attention. Clients need a budget that reflects the reality of a case. When a lawyer flings numbers at a page because he can't be bothered to evaluate what he expects a case to cost, he does his client (and ultimately himself) a disservice.

How Do Realistic Litigation Budgets Help Your Client?

Accurate litigation budgets will enable your client to:

- More closely monitor how the company's financial resources are being utilized;
- Effectively control the costs associated with litigation;
- Adapt to unexpected developments in litigation;
- Report up the ladder with greater confidence about the status of litigation and expectations for cases;
- Establish litigation reserves with greater assurance; and
- Anticipate the effects (whether positive or negative) the litigation and its resolution will have on business operations.[1]

What Does an Effective Litigation Budget Include?

In short, everything. Different clients will have different formats in which they want their budgets submitted. But they are largely seeking the same information. Litigation budgets should capture all the billable hours and litigation expenses that you foresee, usually broken down by tasks. Task-based budgeting structures can be valuable for communicating to your clients the hurdles you expect to encounter in particular cases. Some cases are going to be more discovery-intensive or motion-heavy than others. By providing your clients litigation budgets that reflect the reality of your cases, you can clue them in to these expectations early in the case.

Below is an example of the type of litigation budget you could use for a bodily injury case. It includes most of the tasks I usually expect to encounter through the discovery phase of a case. [Note: The following graph is for demonstrative purposes and does not reflect time spent on any actual cases or billable rates for my firm or me.]

Case Assessment, Development & Administration	Partner Hours	Associate Hours	Paralegal Hours	Total Fees Per Task
Fact Investigation/Development	15.0	5.0		$2,925.00
Analysis/Strategy	15.0	3.0		$2,655.00
Document/File Management	3.0	2.0	10.0	$1,470.00
Settlement/Non-Binding ADR	8.0	1.0	3.0	$1,560.00
Pre-Trial Pleadings and Motions				
Pleadings	3.0			$450.00
Court Mandated Conferences	7.5	5.0		$1,800.00
Dispositive Motions	5.0	5.0		$1,425.00
Other Written Motions and Submissions	3.0	2.0		$720.00
Discovery				
Written Discovery	5.0	5.0		$1,425.00
Document Production	7.5	7.0	10.0	$2,820.00
Depositions	13.0			$1,950.00
Expert Discovery	5.0			$750.00
Discovery Motions	1.5	5.0		$900.00

Does Your Litigation Budget Reflect the Client's Goals?

You should handle litigation in a way that reflects your client's goals and objectives; otherwise, even if you achieve positive results, your client is going to have the impression that he isn't being heard. In the same way, your litigation budgets should reflect how your client likes to handle cases. If they want you to be aggressive with discovery and motion practice, you are likely going to have a higher budget. If the client wants associates and paralegals to do as much work on files as is practical, the budget should reflect that. Litigation budgets are an opportunity to communicate to your client that you are on the same page.

Litigation budgets can serve to reinforce the attorney-client relationship when they are done well. But when a budget does not reflect the realities of a case, it can lead to surprise expenses for the client which he is not prepared to undertake. Clients can prepare to deal with higher budgets, but they find it much more difficult to deal with an unexpectedly high legal bill that requires funds to be pulled from other sources. Your client too is operating on a budget. When you provide a trustworthy litigation budget, you enable his business to operate more effectively.

5

THREE WAYS TO MAKE SURE YOUR CASE
EVALUATIONS ARE USEFUL

I was on the phone with a client when she said to me, you're not going to believe the case evaluation this other lawyer gave me. Now, I have a policy of not speaking badly of my competition, so it appeared that I was about to be entering some choppy waters. Nevertheless, I asked her to tell me about it, mostly because I was curious, but also because, what else was I going to do?

"We've got a construction defect case over in [geographical region omitted] Alabama. There was about $150,000 in claimed damage. This lawyer gave me a case evaluation of between $35,000 and $225,000. But not only that, he didn't give me any explanation. So I called him back and said, 'I need to know how you got to these numbers.' All he told me by way of explanation was, 'We've had some bad verdicts down here recently.'"

There are two problems that we need to address: (1) the case evaluation range was too broad, and (2) it didn't include any data or analysis to support it.

1. Provide Reasonable Case Evaluation Ranges

A key to useful case evaluations is that they be appropriately narrow. Using the example my adjuster relayed to me, there's a pretty big difference between a $35,000 construction defect case and one that's worth $225,000. The purpose of a case evaluation is to arm your client with the information that will allow her to (1) manage her risk, and (2) make an educated decision about resolving the case. An overly broad evaluation does not enable the client to accomplish either of those tasks.

Your knowledge of the practice area; familiarity with the judge, opposing counsel, and the venue; and anecdotal experience with similar cases and the results those yielded are all essential to developing the skill of effectively evaluating cases. There are few things more frustrating than someone who doesn't know how to evaluate a case. It can result in protracted litigation and thousands of dollars being spent unnecessarily.

Below is a sample of eleven cases that I pulled from about three years ago. There are examples of both good evaluations and bad among them. Some are too broad, as in *Jordan v. Johnson*. Others do not reflect where the case ultimately was resolved (but more about this later). For those that are too broad, I didn't provide my client the kind of valuable information that, in retrospect, I could or should have.

Case Name	Settlement/Verdict Amount	Settlement Evaluation	Verdict Evaluation
Duck v. Mouse	$ 24,000.00	$5,000.00-$10,000.00	$20,000.00-$30,000.00
Turtles v. Splinter	$ 60,000.00	$50,000.00-$75,000.00	$100,000.00-$150,000.00
Skywalker v. Vader	$ 200,000.00	$125,000.00-$175,000.00	$150,000.00-$225,000.00
Starling v. Lecter	$ 175,000.00	$125,000.00-$175,000.00	$200,000.00-$300,000.00
Jordan v. Johnson	$ 300,000.00	$100,000.00-$200,000.00	$125,000.00-$250,000.00
Brady v. Manning	$ 50,000.00	$35,000.00-$50,000.00	$50,000.00-$75,000.00
Gates v. Jobs	$ 250,000.00	$210,000.00	$275,000.00-$800,000.00
Shakur v. Naz	$ 715,000.00	$720,000.00-$1,000,000.00	$800,000.00-$925,000.00
Kent v. Wayne	$ 42,500.00	$37,500.00-$75,000.00	$75,000.00-$150,000.00
Lennon v. McCartney	$ 995,131.31	$500,000.00-$750,000.00	$750,000.00-$1,000,000.00
Cobain v. Love	$ 35,000.00	$35,000.00-$50,000.00	$50,000.00-$100,000.00

Evaluating cases can be difficult. Anyone who tells you otherwise is being disingenuous. No two cases are going to develop the same. There is no accounting for what a party might say during depositions. Even if all the lawyers agree on the value of a case, there's no certainty that the defendant will offer the money necessary to get it resolved or that the plaintiff will accept it. Nevertheless it is incumbent upon you to present to your client settlement and verdict evaluation ranges that will enable her to manage her risk and decide whether resolution or continued litigation is her best option.

2. Support Your Case Evaluations with Analysis

Raw numbers are only so useful to a client. They need the reasoning behind your valuation. What are the facts and law that caused you to reach your conclusions? Let's look at the above example again.

> "This lawyer gave me a case evaluation of between $35,000 and $225,000. But not only that, he didn't give me any explanation. So I called him back and said, 'I need to know how you got to these numbers.' All he told me by way of explanation was, 'We've had some bad verdicts down here recently.'"

If you don't support your numbers with analysis, you have not given any authority to your numbers and have given no reason for your client to trust in them. Equally importantly, you haven't given them any way to support their decisions when their boss is evaluating their work.

3. Audit Your Case Evaluations for Accuracy

No matter how narrow or well supported your case evaluations are, they aren't particularly useful to your client if they aren't accurate. This is a difficult thing and can be affected by many factors beyond your control. So any one case may not tell the story, but in the aggregate your case evaluations should show a pattern of cases either settling or trying within the ranges you've identified.

As a part of the above spreadsheet (but not included), I keep a column that reflects the accuracy of my evaluation ranges, with the goal being that I will continue to monitor my results and intentionally improve this skill so as to better serve my clients.

Endeavor to Improve Evaluation Skills

As with any skill, you will only improve your settlement and verdict evaluation skills with intentionality. These are definitely skills worth developing. They serve your interests and your client's. When a client can trust you to help them measure their risk and set reserves on their cases, your relationship will be stronger and the loyalty between you more established.

6

MY WEBSITE GETTING HACKED HELPED ME RELATE TO CLIENTS

L ast year, my website got hacked. Some scoundrel [note: I had to do much editing to choose a non-offensive term for this terrible person, on account of the terrible headache — and expense — that resulted from this episode] dropped some malware into the site and caused all the search result traffic to redirect to a pharmaceutical website. If you plugged a search term into Google that would otherwise bring up a link to one of my blog entries, when you clicked on the link, it took you instead to a website where you could purchase any number of controlled substances online.

I got hacked!

I noticed something was amiss on Saturday, when only thirteen people landed on my site from search results. I was willing to let it go as an anomaly. Weird traffic days happen. But they rarely happen on back-to-back days. So on Sunday when I only got three referrals from search engines, I knew something was wrong. Early Monday morning, I did some investigating and discovered the hack and where all my traffic was going. I freaked out! I went through the five stages of grief in a matter of minutes.

Then I got some bad advice!

I contacted the company that (formerly) hosted my website. They sent me through some steps and promised it would resolve the problem in 24-48 hours. I was really skeptical about everything they'd told me, so I reached out to some bloggers who know more about this than I do. Meanwhile, I was still freaking out. I had *just* launched an ad partnership and was afraid this catastrophe would derail that relationship. Not to mention all the people who were trying to read content on my website, and were winding up on a site where they could buy Valium, Xanax, and whatever else one might need to settle down. Come to think of it, maybe I should have placed an order to settle myself a bit.

It turns out the advice my (former) host gave me was terrible. Not only was it bad advice that would have other potentially adverse consequences, but it wasn't going to solve my existing problem. Not knowing what else to do, I reached back out to the host and got some different advice. They referred me to a company they had an affiliate relationship with who could fix my problem for $300 and a subscription to their security service for $100/mo. No, thanks! My blog doesn't make the kind of money to support that.

Then I got the help I needed.

My desperation was mounting. Not only had it become clear to me this hacking episode was going to pull some money from my pocket, but it had eaten a couple of hours out of my workday, which was less than ideal. I found a security service that got me sorted out at half the fee of the other company and could provide my site security at $10/month. Not only did they fix that problem, I have reached out since then and they've spent a couple hours helping me resolve a different problem that didn't fall within the parameters of our monthly arrangement. They provided for me one of those rare instances of a company going out of its way to help a customer.

Now I'm more sympathetic to my clients.

This brings me to my greater point. My experience of my website getting hacked isn't altogether different from when one of our clients gets sued. When they get served with a complaint, they panic (like I did). They may reach out to a friend to figure out what they need to do (like I did). Not infrequently, they get bad advice (like I did). How many times has a defendant whose case has gone into default told you someone just told them to "Just ignore it — it'll be fine"?

After figuring out the first advice maybe wasn't quite right, they do some searching around and get a referral (like I did). And that's how they end up in your office. Still in a tizzy. Just wanting you to fix the problem. And suddenly realizing this is going to cost them some money (like I did).

At this point, you have a couple of roles to fill: listener and explainer. Your potential client is going to have a lot to get off their chest. Their telling may take the form of anger or sadness. And most of what they tell you will be true ... or at the very least, the truth as they see it. They need someone to hear them out, because they've been through an ordeal.

At the end of their story, it's your job to tell them their ordeal has only just begun. Very rarely do you get to impart good news at this point, because even if there's no real liability and the claims against them are frivolous, it's still going to cost money to get the case dismissed. But you owe them the truth. This is no time to upsell or hide the ball. It is a time for setting expectations, signing a contract for representation, getting paid, and setting about resolving your client's problem.

7

WHO HOLDS THE REINS TO YOUR CONFIDENCE?

N ot long ago, a fellow defense lawyer said to me, "I wish I were as bold and confident as some of the plaintiff lawyers I know. They're so quick to say, 'Fine, let's just try it and see what happens.' Maybe I've been beaten down by too many bad verdicts."

The lawyer who said this is good and experienced. I was surprised to hear him say these things, but once I thought about it, I shouldn't have been. Setting individual personality traits aside, it occurs to me that many of the plaintiff lawyers I know exude more swagger and confidence than their defense counterparts. And there's a good reason for it.

Who Is Holding the Defense Lawyer's Confidence in Check?

By and large, the plaintiff lawyer feels more enabled to act cavalierly about money because every case stands alone. If they get a bad verdict, they've disappointed their client. But in most instances, they've only disappointed one client. They weren't counting on repeat business from the client, only a referral or two down the line hopefully. So while one bad verdict may have taken money out of their pocket, it hasn't affected their overall business structure.

On the contrary, a bad verdict for a defense lawyer may spell the demise of his practice. I know a half dozen or more lawyers this has happened to. Bad verdicts happen to good lawyers. Sometimes that's just how the facts and parties and venue come together, even if you do everything right.

Many defense lawyers rely heavily on one client for the bulk of their business. If they get a bad result for that client who then decides to send its business elsewhere, the defense lawyer's practice will be a shambles and his personal finances may follow closely on its heels. As defense lawyers, our livelihood is at stake with every single case.

You can see then how this can work to hinder how brashly or cavalierly a lawyer might manage his cases. But there is a problem with this way of thinking. While fear can be a good motivator, being driven by fear and worry about what is beyond our control can paralyze us. Regardless, there has to be a better solution to this problem than me saying, "Don't worry about it. Your business isn't going to collapse ... probably." And indeed, I think there is a solution.

Establish Stronger Relationships through Effective Communication

There was a time when corporate clients and law firms worked together with unquestioned loyalty for years or even decades. Corporate executives and in-house counsel went hunting and fishing with their lawyers and were generally wined and dined. Lawyers overbilled their files. And everyone was generally happy.

Then came the age of big data and metrics, where companies began to audit files and examine where their money was going. What they discovered was a lot of their money was going to outside counsel, who were not being good stewards of their clients' financial resources. This led to an era of mistrust and a general lack of loyalty.

We need to get back to an era of trust. Not a false trust founded in complicity in being wooed by fancy restaurants and hunting lodges. But rather a trust established by communication, efficient representation, and effective results. There are many facets of communication that make the attorney-client relationship healthier, and you are reading in this book about several of them. Litigation costs and risk analysis. Compliance with reporting guidelines and timely updates even beyond the guidelines. All of these are important aspects of communication with your client that establishes a rapport and effectuates loyalty.

When your relationships with clients are built upon a foundation of solid work-product and effective communication, there is a mutual respect that is less likely to dissipate with a singular bad result or by a change in the prevailing winds. Strong relationships supported by effective communication can embolden you to take measured risks and exhibit the confidence and cavalier posture you see in others.

8

LAW FIRM MARKETING MYTHS: MARKETING IS FOR EXTROVERTS

As you have just read, marketing has long been done by wining and dining clients and potential clients. Wining and dining is the preference of extroverts. Those personalities who thrive on engagement with others. It has been the way of the world for decades. And there is still a place for that, but there are also plenty of other marketing methods available to us now. And by *us*, I mean introverts.

What is an introvert, and am I one of them?

There is a bit of a stigma attached to the word *introvert*. Upon hearing it, people sometimes envision hermits who would just as soon never see or interact with another human. That's rather a misconception. As with most things, there are degrees of introversion and extroversion. In fact you may be wondering now where you fit.

Here's a question that may help shed some light on the matter: When you've been around a large group of people for an evening, how do you feel afterward? If your batteries are fully charged and you'd like nothing more than to talk with someone and share your experience, you are likely an extrovert. If toward the end of the evening, all you can think about is curling into your favorite chair and reading a book because you are feeling drained with all the interaction and stimulation, you are likely an introvert.

Susan Cain writes in *Quiet: The Power of Introverts in a World That Can't Stop Talking* that introverts "may have strong social skills and enjoy parties and business meetings, but after a while wish they were home in their pajamas. They prefer to devote their social energies to close friends, colleagues, and family. They listen more than they talk, think before they speak, and often feel as if they express themselves better in writing than in conversation. They tend to dislike conflict. Many have a horror of small talk, but enjoy deep discussions."[1]

I am squarely in the latter camp. I'm not particularly shy, and I don't mind group events (although I wouldn't go so far as to say I look forward to them), but afterward I am mentally wiped out. When I am looking at an upcoming conference, speaking engagement, or client dinner, I have to mentally prepare myself. But most important, I try to make sure that the day or two after the event requires little socialization. My batteries need recharging. The best way for me to do that is to disengage from social interaction.

I was recently at a business dinner. There were only four of us eating together, but it was coming on the heels of three inter-active-intensive days. And I was drained. After about thirty minutes, I started checking my watch. The company was good, and I liked the people I was with, but in that moment, I wanted nothing more than to get away. I needed to decompress. I couldn't do that with people around.

Law firm marketing is for introverts too

If you are an introvert hoping I will tell you there is a way to market yourself to potential new clients that doesn't require you to get out of your quiet comfort zone, you are going to be disappointed. If people are going to trust you enough to send you work, you will have to get in front of them and build up some trust equity. Consider what Susan Cain had to say long these lines:

> Figure out what you are meant to contribute to the world and make sure you contribute it. If this requires public speaking or networking or other activities that make you uncomfortable, do them anyway. But accept that they're difficult, get the training you need to make them easier, and reward yourself when you're done. Here's a rule of thumb for networking events: one new honest-to-goodness relationship is worth ten fistfuls of business cards. Rush home afterward and kick back on your sofa. Carve out restorative niches.[2]

There are some things you can do to make going outside your comfort zones easier on yourself. If you aren't very good at small talk, read tips for having good conversations before going to a networking event. For example, people really enjoy talking about themselves. You can have a conversation with a stranger in which you start by asking him what he does for a living and stay engaged in the conversation by asking natural, follow-up questions. When you two part ways, he's going to think you just had the greatest interaction, and you are going to realize you only had to speak a couple dozen words and he did all the work by talking about a topic he enjoys – himself.

There are plenty of other things you can do to improve your marketing without increasing your interaction. This was part of my motivation for starting a law blog in June of 2016. The blog enabled me to provide information and valuable content to clients and potential new clients in a way that would develop trust equity. They would learn about me and what I could do to help them without me having to sell them on it.

There are other things I do to provide value to clients and people with whom I have relationships that may not be clients. If I write something on a substantive legal issue that may affect a client, I'll send it to them. This has a two-fold effect: it provides a service to my client by making them aware of a development in their field that could affect their business, and it keeps me fresh in their mind in case a problem arises.

Think about the things you can do to add value and build up trust equity with clients and potential clients. There is so much more to effective marketing than wining, dining, and entertaining. I cannot overstate the value in providing real substance and developing trusting, mutually beneficial relationships.

9

LAW FIRM MARKETING MYTHS: MARKETING MEANS TELLING CLIENTS HOW GREAT YOU ARE

Y our potential clients do not need to know how great you are. They could not care less about where you went to law school or how high falutin' you are. Among other things, this emphasis on the wrong things is what lawyers get so wrong with their websites (more on this later) and marketing efforts. Clients need to know what you can do for them. They need to know they can trust you to handle their business efficiently and effectively. They need you to be a good steward of your time and their money.

When potential clients are considering doing business with you, there are certain things you need to address to put them at ease, earning their trust and their business. Here are three questions potential clients need you to answer:

1. Is your proposal interesting to them?

Potential clients often answer the question of whether your proposal is interesting to them before ever contacting you. If the answer is no, then you will likely not hear from them. Your potential clients are deciding whether your proposal is interesting based on the marketing materials they first encounter from your firm. Maybe that's your website, a billboard, or an industry publication. If you fail to identify the problem they're experiencing, and how you can guide them to the solution, you've already lost.

To be effective, you have to know who your potential client is. If you have misidentified the people who are interested in your services or the services they are in need of, you will be unable to correctly identify for them the problem they are experiencing. You will not be effectively communicating that you understand what they are experience and have the knowledge and skills to guide them to a resolution.

But if you have correctly identified your potential client and their problem, you will get their attention. Once you have their attention, you need to distinguish yourself from others who are seeking their business. You can accomplish that in part by establishing that your proposal is the one that best meets their needs.

2. Is your proposal right for them?

Here's a story that a young lawyer shared with me about an experience she had: Before this lawyer had enough experience and gray hair to go to potential client meetings on her own, she made contact with an insurance company who was interested in her firm doing their work. So she set up the meeting that the managing partner and she were to attend. By the day of the meeting, a couple more lawyers had tagged along.

One of the partners had it in his head to talk about one particular line of business the potential new client wrote, and how experienced their firm was in handling it. The client wasn't interested in talking about that. They wanted to talk about bigger picture items. Yet the partner would not be dissuaded. At every turn of the meeting, he brought the conversation back to what he had come their to say.

The rest of the lawyers in attendance were horrified. But the offending partner was oblivious. And short of handing him a note bearing some very direct message, there seemed no way to derail the train. So on it went.

For you to answer a potential client's question as to whether your proposal is right for their needs, you must actively listen to discern their needs. This may require you to disregard any presuppositions you brought with you to the meeting. Otherwise, you will be answering the wrong question.

3. Can they trust you?

Trust is hard won but easily lost. A trust relationship takes time to build but you can certainly signal right away that you cannot be trusted. Some of the most effective ways to communicate from the outset are to oversell yourself, be unduly critical of your competition, and fudge on facts.

Carry yourself with integrity and deal with everyone in an upright manner. There is a shortage of people who are genuine and honest. Being someone known for these characteristics will open doors for you that would otherwise have been closed. It will give people the confidence to take their interactions with you at face value.

10

LAW FIRM MARKETING MYTHS: "JUST DO GREAT WORK"

ow many times have you heard something to this effect: "The key to getting clients is to just do great work." Well, I'm here to tell you that's a partial truth, at best.

Clients expect you to do great work.

Clients *expect* great work. That's what happens when they pay upwards of $150/hour for someone's services (and most times 2-3 times that amount). There are built-in expectations. So the expression that if you *just* do great work, you will get more clients, is mostly inaccurate. The reality is, if you *just* do great work, you'll be ... meeting expectations. And nobody refers their friends, family, and coworkers to businesses who *just* meet their expectations.

It is important that you be a good lawyer and do great work for your clients. But you cannot rely on doing great work as a means of bringing in more business. Consider this account from a defense lawyer who has had experience with the theory that all you need for business to come your way is to just do great work:

> I was at a midsized civil defense firm at one point. They basically had this marketing strategy that you just had to do great work. Eighty percent of the firm's work was from one client. They did very well. Then the client made some internal shifts, and the firm really had a decline in work and ended up scrambling to start marketing.
>
> While great work does help bring in clients, I don't think it is at an appreciable rate. It's just luck at that point. You have to make sure you are on potential clients' radars, and doing that at a steady rate is better than not at all and then trying to play catch-up if something goes south.
>
> That firm shrank from about twenty-five attorneys to ten. I think they are back around fifteen now over a five-year period. Now their strategy includes regular marketing efforts.
>
> My current firm is very much do great work and other work will come in, but they also encourage marketing, even if in small amounts. And from what I understand of the firm's history, they have not had the size and business fluctuations the other firm had.

Combine great work with other marketing efforts

Here is the truth about doing great work for your clients – if you combine that with other marketing efforts, you can leverage yourself into a better situation. For most lawyers, clients aren't going to come find you.

For all the work I've brought into my firm, none of it has been because some company came calling: "Hey, Jeremy, we heard you're a good lawyer and you really make a priority of client communication and collaboration. And we've just got to add you as our panel counsel." Nope. It might happen once in a while. But it's not something you can count on.

You have to find ways to meet people who may send you business. You have to begin to build up trust with those people and add value for them. Then perhaps when they have a need, they will think of you and send you work. Then the great work you are doing will result in them continuing to send you work and be your client.

Doing great work will help you maintain your existing clients, and it *may* result in those clients recommending you to others, but *just* doing great work should not to be relied upon as the core marketing strategy for your firm.

11

WHERE LAW FIRM WEBSITES GO WRONG
AND HOW TO FIX IT

I f you go to most law firm websites, they spend the majority of their space telling you how great the firm is, how accomplished their lawyers are, and how extraordinary their results have been. This is were law firm websites go wrong. There is a common misconception that by telling our clients and prospective clients how great we are, they will be more inclined to work with us. For example, here is how my bio read on our firm website in the earliest years of my practice:

> Jeremy W. Richter graduated cum laude from Tennessee Temple University with a Bachelor of Science in Secondary Education in 2004. He then moved to Birmingham to teach and coach at Tabernacle Christian School. Concurrent with his employment there, he earned a Master of Art degree in History at the University of Alabama at Birmingham in 2007.
>
> In 2012, Mr. Richter earned his Juris Doctor from Samford University's Cumberland School of Law, where he received the Spirit of Service Award and was the Scholar of Merit for

Special Topics in Environmental Law. Mr. Richter began his practice at Webster Henry in October 2012. He resides in Birmingham with his wife Anna and son Jack, where they attend Gardendale First Baptist Church.

But clients and potential clients don't care what you did in law school five or twenty-five years ago. By and large, your pedigree is of little consequence to them. Clients are not convinced to work with you because of these things. Your past accomplishments do not address potential clients' concerns. Where law firm websites go wrong is that they are making their websites and their communication about *themselves*.

The Solution to the Problem of Ineffective Law Firm Websites

What you should be doing instead is making your website about your client. Your potential client has a problem, or else they would not be seeking out your services. They have invented a new piece of tech and need a patent. They've been sued for divorce. They've been injured in a car wreck. Or they may have a problem they are not even sure how to verbalize. If all your website does is tell your client how great you are, it doesn't address their problem.

Your client may need you to help them identify their problem, but that's not all. They also need to know that you can help them resolve their problem. According to Donald Miller in *Building a StoryBrand*, one of the most common mistakes businesses make is failing to focus on what they can offer that will help their customers both survive and thrive: "The key is to make your company's message about something that helps the customer survive."[1]

Potential clients may hear about your firm through word of

mouth or social media, but they go to your website to learn more. When they get there "their hopes need to be confirmed, and they need to be convinced we have a solution to their problem."[2] You can't possibly convince potential clients you have the solution to their problems if all your website tells them is that you participated in a moot court competition fifteen years ago and were the editor of the law review. "The customer simply needs to know that you have something they want and you can be trusted to deliver whatever that is."[3]

How I've Attempted to Address the Problem

In my bio on my firm's website, I want clients and potential clients to understand what they can expect from me and how I like for us to work together:

> When approaching cases, my priority is to collaborate with clients to achieve efficient and effective results by way of tenacious advocacy. I strive to align my tactics and objectives with my client's goals in handling cases. I enjoy the various aspects of litigation, ranging from strategy and planning that go into research and brief writing, to the in-person chess matches that take place during depositions and trial. It is important to me to keep my clients and myself informed of trends and developments in Alabama law, so we can most effectively evaluate and prosecute cases to the best possible result. To that end, I regularly write articles in trade publications and author a law blog that focuses on insurance defense and practice/case management topics.

We are in a competitive industry. We need to turn every resource to our advantage. Your website is frequently the first face of your company that many potential clients will see. If you are failing to adequately communicate with potential clients on your website, you may never have the opportunity to represent them and resolve their problem. Be sure your website identifies your potential clients' problems for them and tells them how you can address it, rather than telling them how awesome you are.

PART II

CASE MANAGEMENT

EXPLORE SOLUTIONS BY THINKING LIKE A CHILD

I n his novel *The Ocean at the End of the Lane*, Neil Gaiman writes, "Adults follow paths. Children explore." When facing a problem, it is easier for us to follow in the steps of those who have come before us than to explore and seek out creative solutions. But it is not uncommon that the "tried and true" solutions whose paths we are following aren't as great as we envision them to be.

Have you ever read a franchise agreement or other business contract? Most of them were originally drafted a decade ago. Since then, new contributors have added paragraphs and bullet points as new situations have arisen. Nothing ever gets deleted. There may even be conflicting language. By the time you start using the time-tested template, the contract is so unnecessarily complex and imposing that you can barely understand it, much less explain everything to your client. This is what comes of mindlessly following the paths before us.

Explore Your Options Like a Child

As I entered my fourth year of practice in 2016, I was approaching a crossroad. I was either going to continue to be just a good associate (and good associates are a dime a dozen) or I was going to take steps to position myself to be made a partner within the next couple of years. I needed to develop my own business and make myself invaluable. As it stood at the time, I had plenty of work to do, but it was someone's else's work and someone else's clients. I needed to put things in motion to effectuate a change. But what? And how?

The well-worn path was to go to mega-conferences focused on your practice areas and try to rub elbows with people who might in the future send you business. I did that a couple of times and decided that tactic wasn't going to work for me, at least not as my only marketing effort. I still go to conferences, but smaller conferences, and have found a way to do the home-work to make those opportunities worth my while.

I had to engage some childlike creativity to find a solution that worked for me. I put a great deal of thought into things and assessed my strengths and weaknesses. Major weakness: I'm an introvert who does not enjoy small talk and hordes of people. Major strength: I enjoy writing.

For me then the new path I wanted to explore was blogging. Having a law blog has kept me engaged in developments in my practice areas and within the business of law that I did not previously experience. I have developed relationships and opportunities that would not otherwise have surfaced. My first book, *Building a Better Practice*, directly resulted from the blog. All this writing has given me opportunities to provide information and data to clients and potential clients, which helps build trust equity.

I can't tell you I have clients now as a direct result of my deviation from the standard path. But I have developed confidence and a platform I would not have had without exploring another option.

Don't Limit Your Exploration Application

Engaging your childlike curiosity is not limited to any one particular part of your practice. You can get creative in your motion practice, in considering arguments to be made in support of your positions, in business and financial planning, and of course in marketing. While the well-worn paths may serve their purposes, you will not know what other, and perhaps better, opportunities await you, unless you deviate from the path and explore.

CHALLENGE CONVENTIONAL APPROACHES

M alcolm Gladwell's *David and Goliath* begins by telling the well-known story of, you guessed it, David and Goliath. But in the book, he reframes the story, which he asserts we have been misinterpreting.

Reinterpreting What an Underdog Is

This is not the story of a small shepherd boy who went to war with an outsized opponent and happened to win. Instead the story of David and Goliath is one of a small shepherd boy who refused to concede to the conventional warfare his opponent was demanding.

The shepherd assessed the giant's strengths and weaknesses and determined that he was unable to defeat the giant on his own terms. David then analyzed his own strengths. In the fields protecting his sheep, he had honed his skills with the sling. He had slain a lion and a bear by this method when they carried off one of his charges. Scientific studies have determined that a skilled slinger could release a stone with the same force as a large-caliber handgun. This sling was a weapon of war, the artillery weapon that preceded the bow.

When David met Goliath in the valley for a battle to the death, Goliath had three weapons and was clad in armor. He was prepared for close-hand combat. But David refused to meet Goliath on the giant's own terms. Neither Goliath nor the Philistine army knew it at that moment, but they had already lost the battle. Goliath was too heavy and slow-moving to react to David's method of attack.

After descending into the valley to meet Goliath, David addressed him:

> "You come to me with a sword and with a spear and with a javelin, but I come to you in the name of the Lord of hosts, the God of the armies of Israel, whom you have defied. This day the Lord will deliver you into my hand, and I will strike you down and cut off your head. And I will give the dead bodies of the host of the Philistines this day to the birds of the air and to the wild beasts of the earth, that all the earth may know that there is a God in Israel, and that all this assembly may know that the Lord saves not with sword and spear. For the battle is the Lord's, and he will give you into our hand." I Samuel 17:44-47 (ESV).

David began running toward Goliath while whirling his sling. He let go of the rope and launched a projectile toward his enemy at his only vulnerable point. Less than one second later, the stone embedded itself in the giant's skull rendering him either unconscious or dead. The shepherd then grabbed the giant's sword and cut off his head.

David defeated his opponent by challenging convention and refusing to meet him on Goliath's own terms. By choosing a different strategy, David turned the odds in his own favor. His opponent did not recognize the danger he was in and was unable to defend himself against an unanticipated form of battle.

Choosing to Play 4-on-5

When I was in 10th grade, our basketball team was playing a school, Metro, against whom we were pretty evenly matched. We did not have one particularly good player, but had several moderately good players. Metro, on the other hand, had one good player, while the rest of the team was made up of non-difference makers. My coach understood that if we played a conventional game, the odds of victory were in doubt, so he devised a plan.

I was not a good offensive player. But I loved defense, and I was a good defender. I relished the opportunity to hassle the opposing point guard. If I could get a five-second call on him at the top of the key, it was a mountain-top experience. I envisioned myself as a white, suburban, 135-pound Gary Payton. What I lacked in talent (and mind you, there was very little talent), I tried to compensate for with tenacity.

In the pre-game meeting, the coach instructed me: "Jeremy, I want you to play defense on #25 the whole game. When we're on offense. When we're on defense. I want you to tell me what kind of gum he's chewing, what kind of deodorant he wears. You stick on him the whole game. You'll get in his head." I've rarely smiled so broadly. This was to be my finest hour.

I did as instructed. When we were in man defense, I was on him. When we went to a box-and-one, I defended #25. When we were on offense and #25 was guarding our best player, I was glued to his hip. It didn't take long for him to realize things were not occurring in the traditional way. He started trash talking and getting frustrated. His foul total started to accumulate, and his productivity decreased. The score was becoming lopsided in our favor. In the third quarter, #25 drew his fifth and final foul when, out of frustration, he shoved me and said some not nice things. The game was not much of a contest after that.

By challenging conventions, my coach had put our opponent on their heels and attacked them with a strategy for which they were unprepared. He gave us the advantage by electing to put his offense at a strategic disadvantage.

Refuse to Play Your Opponent's Conventional Game

When you're litigating cases, there are going to be times you know the deck stacks against you. Either there are bad facts or bad law, and if you don't do something extraordinary, your client is going to lose. These are times when you may need to consider not meeting your opponent where she's at, but rather begin playing a different game.

Consider this scenario: Opposing counsel has an expert who is going to testify that your client is liable for the plaintiff's injuries. You take the expert's deposition and discover there are some holes in his opinions and analysis. The conventional thing to do is to get your own expert who will testify that your client is not liable. This is what your opponent likely expects you to do.

An alternative approach is to hire no expert of your own. You may choose instead just to poke holes in the opinions and analysis given by your opponent's expert. What is wrong with his calculations? Why could the accident not have occurred as he is asserting? What facts has he failed to consider or evidence is he omitting?

Do not comply with conventional approaches as a matter of course. Take a broad view of your case and consider all of the possible strategies available to you. Get an outside perspective that may shed light on a tactic you had not considered. Do not concede to fighting in the manner your opponent is demanding. Devise a strategy that is most effective for reaching your goals, and execute it. Leave your opponent standing flat-footed, wondering what you are doing as you sprint toward them and unleash the stone that will topple the giant.

14

FRAME YOUR DAILY TASKS IN A MORE PRODUCTIVE LIGHT

I keep two 5x8 notebooks with me at all times: one white and one yellow – I'll tell you about them briefly now and expound on this later.[1] These allow my mind to rest a little more easily. If I were to lose them, I'd be in a heap of trouble. The yellow one contains all of my daily billable time entries, and I have every one dating back to my very first day of practice. I'll admit to being oddly sentimental about them. But my wife would likely tell you I'm both odd and sentimental about a good many things.

The white notebook contains my to-do list, which is usually 2-3 pages long at any given time. I also have each and every one of these that I've filled up with tasks to be completed. But here's the thing about my to-do list — it contains many tasks to be completed that I'm not too keen on and never envisioned were a part of practicing law. In fact, some of my daily tasks are downright unenjoyable, especially the ones that read, "Make phone call to ...." There are days I'd rather take a punch from Kimbo Slice than make a bunch of phone calls. But they're important(ish) and have to be done. So it occasionally helps to frame things in a different context to provide motivation to do the tasks.

Frame it in a motivational context

I write a lot of reports for clients. I mean, dozens per month. And it gets tiresome. But the reporting is important. And what's important to the client needs to carry the same weight for me, but that doesn't make it any more enjoyable. So sometimes it helps to put things in a different context.

For example, I have several reports to write, but I'm really tired of writing reports. If I write the report, my client will be well informed about the case and will be happy. If my client is happy, he's going to continue to send me work. If my client continues to send me work, I will keep building my practice. If I build a successful practice, I can provide for my family. So by writing this report, I am providing a better life for my family. Of course, it is kind of absurd, but that doesn't make it less motivating.

Frame it as following orders

There are myriad forms of motivation. As a lawyer (as in many other walks of life), we have to make a lot of phone calls. A friend of mine *hated* calling people on the phone, but her managing partner believed that phone calls were more effective than emails, and the phone was his preferred method of communication. His standing order whenever communication was needed was, "Just pick up the phone and call them."

My friend then, whenever she needed to make a call, would tell herself, "I have to call this person because Partner told me to." This worked for her because she is a self-professed rule-follower, which was sufficient motivation for her to attend to that task. She is clearly a more compliant person than I am. I, on the other hand, would have taken that instruction as a recommendation and continued to find a different workaround rather than having unnecessary human interaction.

Frame daily tasks as serving a greater purpose

Most of your daily tasks are not an end unto themselves. They serve a broader purpose, no matter how inane the individual task. Perhaps it is case development or managing client relationships. Or maybe it is in furtherance or growing your practice and finding new clients.

Every day, I get a list of all the lawsuits that have been filed in Alabama. So I set aside time every few days to check the lists to see if any of my clients or their insureds have been sued and may need to be made aware of it. Most days, this chore is fruitless. But it is a task that my clients appreciate when something does come up unexpectedly. So I maintain the practice because it serves the greater goal of serving my clients.

You likely have dozens of daily tasks that, of themselves, are not rewarding. But regardless, they must be attended to. Don't shy away from employing whatever mind games are necessary to get your tasks done.

15

APPLYING THE WAIT PRINCIPLE WHEN ADDRESSING THE JURY

W hen addressing a jury, lawyers can often get carried away with the sound of their own voice. Talking for the sake of talking. Continuing to be the center of attention because you're under the impression the jury cares what you have to say or will be more likely to find in your client's favor the longer you talk to them.

This is a bad strategy. Whenever you are in front of a jury, you need to have reasons you're talking, goals to achieve. One way to do this is to apply the WAIT Principle.

WAIT - Why Am I Talking?

The WAIT principle can help you be more discerning about what you're saying and why you're saying it. If you are talking in front of a jury, there should be a tactical consideration behind it. This applies whether you are asking questions of the jury panel in voir dire, speaking directly to the jury in opening statements or closing arguments, examining witnesses, or making objections.

In a recent trial, plaintiff's counsel voir dired the jury for more than two hours. He was certainly thorough, and he got a good deal of information from the jury panel, but it was exhausting. When my partner stood up to begin her voir dire, you could see the panel deflate.

She remarked, "I feel like we've already heard plaintiff's opening statement." This drew a few laughs and more head nods. My partner then asked about fifteen minutes worth of essential questions.

She pulled herself up short in mid thought and asked the potential jurors, "Can we all just agree that we won't form any opinions about what happened until we've heard the evidence?" The juror's relief was audible.

When you are contemplating your communications with your audience, you want to be purposeful to achieve the best results. The WAIT principle gives a structural framework for effective and considered communication. Here are four questions you should ask of yourself that will help guide how you choose to communicate:

- Am I talking because I want to share something that I think is relevant to the conversation?
- Am I talking to control the narrative?
- Am I talking to garner sympathy?
- Am I talking because I want to be the center of attention?

Each of these reasons for talking has its merits, and in the appropriate context can be effective.

1. Am I talking because I want to share something that I think is relevant to the case?

Any time you are speaking in the presence of a jury, what you're saying should be relevant to the case. Even if you are sharing a parable or using a metaphor, if it isn't clearly applicable to the facts, law, or theme of the case, then the jury will get disinterested or worse ... confused.

In this era of ever-present distraction and shorter attention spans, keeping an audience's attention is difficult. The best ways to maintain the audience's interest is through storytelling and providing useful information that drives the case forward.

2. Am I talking to control the narrative?

Your communication must be directed and intentional. There will be times in trials where the only reason you are addressing certain topics is to control the narrative. If you are trying a disputed liability car-wreck case, you want the jury to believe your client's account of the accident.

You begin this with the way you formulate and ask questions in voir dire. You continue to manage the jury's perspective of the incident by the manner in which you inform them during opening statements. The questions you ask of witnesses should be directed to controlling the narrative you are tailoring. Your closing argument should be constructed in such a manner that all the prior elements of the case are sewn together so the jury reaches an inevitable conclusion of finding for your client.

3. Am I talking to garner sympathy (or erode it)?

In a trial a couple of years ago, my partner and I were defending a case in which we were not disputing liability for a car wreck. The plaintiff was not at fault. The at-fault driver had already settled out of the case. We were representing the insurance company against whom the plaintiff was trying to recover uninsured/underinsured benefits. We agreed that he was entitled to some amount of money, but we firmly believed (and the jury eventually agreed) that the plaintiff was over-reaching. He was claiming to be more injured than we believed him to be.

My objective in cross-examining the plaintiff was to erode the sympathy that his lawyer was trying to establish. During direct examination, the plaintiff talked all about his chronic pain and how much he missed racing motorcycles, which he claimed to be unable to do since the accident. The trouble for them was, I had photographs of him racing motorcycles after the accident.

All of my questions were intended to paint him in a corner so that I could impeach his testimony. I had a strategy going in rather than scatter shooting and hoping to land a few points. If I were able to impeach him and show him to be less injured than he was claiming, I could get a step closer to getting a favorable verdict from the jury.

4. Am I talking because I want to be the center of attention?

Mostly, if you are talking just to be the center of attention, you will be on treacherous ground. However, I have seen this tactic used effectively by a grizzled veteran in a dangerous venue. We were trying a case where (again) we were arguing the Plaintiff's neck surgery she had three years after the accident wasn't made necessary by the accident, and we had some pretty good evidence to support that. In closing arguments, my partner told a story about when he was a child and got a spanking for something he didn't do. His point to the jury was that if they attributed the neck surgery to the accident and awarded damages to the plaintiff accordingly, they would be spanking our client for something he didn't do.

When the plaintiff's lawyer got up for his rebuttal, he preached to that jury. He must have told that jury to "Spank him" four dozen times. It was a more fiery invocation than I've seen in most churches. He was making himself the center of attention, but doing so in such a compelling way that the jury fed on it.

The WAIT Principle requires intentionality

Why am I talking? Have a purpose for everything you say and do in front of a jury. In the same way that a good novelist only includes the parts of a story that drive his characters and plot forward, everything you do in front of the jury should be measured and intended to drive your case toward the jury finding in your client's favor.

16

VOIR DIRE IS HARD

A RECENT TRIAL EXPERIENCE

S etting: *A rural, conservative gem of a county in middle Alabama. Plaintiff's counsel is with one of the more well-known personal injury firms in Alabama. The plaintiff himself is a dullard of a fellow, who poses me no danger of charming the jury. The judge is a charismatic guy who is wisely using this opportunity to allow his captive constituents to get to know him and the other elected civic officials in the county. The judge delivers his opening remarks and allows the jurors who believe they should excuse from service to present themselves and their excuses (which are largely ... hogwash), and he excuses them one and all. It is time to voir dire the jury.*

Counsel for the plaintiff gets to voir dire the jury first. He has a chance to charm them and impress upon them his theory of the case. He gets to ask questions that evoke their sympathy. They may commiserate with the plaintiff because they too have had chronic back problems. Of course, the jury may be a hardened lot and not empathetic about the plaintiff's back problem. In this instance, several jurors suffered from back pain, but they weren't taking opioid pain medication and they weren't considering undergoing surgery. These jurors were just going about their lives dealing with their issues.

The accident that was the subject of this case occurred when a woman pulled out in front of the plaintiff while he was driving his motorcycle. He struck the side of her vehicle and cartwheeled over the top until he eventually collided with the pavement. There were several jurors in the panel who rode motorcycles and were sympathetic with the plight of drivers not seeing or even looking for motorcycles.

As plaintiff's counsel continued to voir dire the jury, he had to take one issue head-on, or it might appear he was hiding from it: he worked for a giant TV-advertising, billboard-placing plaintiff's firm. How did the jury feel about that? Oh, they had *strong* feelings about it! Too many ads. Too much litigation. Personal injury commercials are all you see on daytime television. Those who didn't speak up were nodding in affirmation. The lawyer knew this was coming, but the plaintiff himself slid lower in his chair with every response. In spite of this, everyone said they could and would be fair to the plaintiff.

The plaintiff had already settled his claims with the lady who had pulled out in front of him. Our trial was over whether he was entitled to any underinsured motorist benefits, and if so, how much. The plaintiff may have been disadvantaged because his lawyer's firm is seen on televisions and billboards across the state, but I was representing an insurance company. There are few disadvantages greater than that in civil litigation. No one likes paying insurance premiums and most everyone has had a bad experience with an insurance company. I started my voir dire off by introducing myself and my corporate representative. I wanted to personalize us both. I made a joke; it fell flat.

My second disadvantage was that by this time, we were approaching lunch time. When you're working against the clock like this, you have to be precise and direct. There's no room for redundant questions and wasting time. With most of the interesting and conversational topics already taken, I set into a series of questions about insurance companies, insurance claims, bad experiences with insurance companies, and biases against my client. It was dull but necessary. My questions were drawing no responses from anyone, except the older gentleman who hated all of us. The non-responsiveness was both good and bad. No one was apparently going to hold against my client the fact that it was an insurance company, but I sure wasn't getting a chance to establish a rapport with the jury.

After I asked my questions, I sat down. Over the next thirty minutes we struck our jury and dismissed for lunch. The case settled during lunch, which was somewhat a disappointment. I'd worked all weekend only to put the landing gear down after we'd barely gotten off the ground.

The next day, my partner and I sat down to debrief the case. I expressed that I felt during voir dire that I had exhibited as much personality as our beige office walls. She said she feels that way every time she has to voir dire a jury in an uninsured/ underinsured motorist case. The questions are dry and largely impersonal, but we have to obtain the information. It only gets a little spicy when you have an old guy who hates everyone and wants to air his lifetime of grievances.

It is difficult to effectively voir dire a jury. To improve your chances, you need to have a theme, a plan, and know your material. And you'll need to insert just a little personality into it as well.

17

SHOULD YOUR OPENING STATEMENTS BE PLANNED OUT OR EXTEMPORANEOUS?

I
f voir dire is important because it is the first opportunity the jury has to get to know you, opening statements are important because they are your first opportunity to tell the jury what your case is about. If you do it effectively, you can clue the jury in on the important facts and evidence while capturing their attention. But if you're ineffective, you will set the tone for a boring experience and lose a valuable chance to enable the jury to connect with your client.

Whether opening statements should be written out or extemporaneous

Before going to law school, I taught high school for six years. In the education realm, there is a lot of emphasis on daily lesson plans and writing out goals and objectives. At the time, I didn't find much value in those things, but over the years, written goals have become increasingly important to me, and I've found that shooting from the hip can have its limitations.

When I'm preparing for trial, I usually outline what I want to talk about or just bullet-point certain lines that I want to make sure to say. There's a lot of time and energy that goes into it, but on paper, it doesn't usually look like much. I don't get stage fright — years of teaching high schoolers will make you hardened to such things — so I'm not usually in any real danger of all my thoughts fleeing from me. But I don't want to forget an important detail due to an oversight either.

In the example below, my opening would be pretty short. I wanted to capture the jury's attention with my brevity and signal to them there wasn't much to this case.

An Outlined Opening Statement

- Thank them for their service and willingness to participate in this very important process.
- This is a case where we agree on everything except one issue: money.
- There is no dispute about the accident — the plaintiff was not at fault for the accident. A lady named Ms. Tortfeasor was at fault.
- There is no dispute about the plaintiff's medical treatment. He went to the ER shortly after the accident to get checked out. After they checked him out, they released him on the same day.
- No dispute that he had a pre-existing back injury and leg pain before this accident that had nothing to do with this accident.
- No dispute that the plaintiff is entitled to something for the discomfort he endured after the accident.
- We just can't agree on how much the plaintiff is entitled to. That's what we need you all for.
- I expect that once you have heard the testimony, you'll find that the plaintiff has not had treatment for injuries related to this accident in over 2 years.
- The only treatment he continues to receive is for the

arthritis, back pain, and leg pain that he had before this accident. He is taking the same pain medication and anti-anxiety medications that he took before this accident.

- Plaintiff is riding motorcycles again like he was before the accident. He's wearing the same helmet and gloves he was wearing on the day this accident occurred.

- I'm confident that after you've heard the testimony and once you consider the evidence, you will come to a consensus and will render a just, reasonable verdict.

A well-planned and written out opening statement

But for my most recent trial, I wanted to try something different. I wrote out the entire opening in paragraph form as if I were writing a story. I figured I would then reduce it to my usual outline before trial, because the paragraph format was too dense and long for me to take up to the lectern. I enjoyed writing everything out in long form, and it made me even more comfortable with the material than just outlining or bullet-pointing everything. Here's what that looked like for me:

A Written Opening Statement

I have a rambunctious 3-year-old son. He is all energy all the time. Whenever we go into a nice store with breakable things, the owner eyes us from behind the counter, and I'm holding my breath the whole time we're in there. I always kneel down in front of Jack and tell him, "Look at me. You have to be super careful in here. Because if you break something, you have to buy it." And that's fair. We've all heard that before — you break it you buy it. That's the way it should be?

But what if Jack and I went into a Hallmark store and all their nice ceramic things were already lying in the floor broken? Should we have to buy the things that someone else broke? No, of course not.

Or what if someone comes in after Jack and I leave and they break one of those "Precious Moments" or Kim Anderson figurines? Then the store owner calls me to tell me I need to pay for something that someone who came after me broke? I'll probably tell him to get lost. Because that's not right. You should pay for the things you break. You shouldn't have to pay for the things other people break.

But that's what the Plaintiff is asking you, the jury, for. The Plaintiff is asking you to make my client pay for things she didn't break.

We don't dispute that my client ran into the back of the Plaintiff's truck. I expect the evidence is going to show that it had been raining that day. She was on her way home from work. As she approached a rise in the road, she checked the clock on her dash. My client came over the hill and when she saw the brake lights of the Plaintiff's vehicle, she applied her brakes. The brakes locked and her tires slid on the wet road and she slid into the back of the Plaintiff's vehicle.

You're going to hear the Plaintiff tell you that she initially had some neck and back pain from this accident, but that went away. She'll tell you that she has arthritis in her neck and back, and she has back and neck pain sometimes.

I expect the Plaintiff is going to tell you the only real lasting injury from this accident is a rotator cuff tear in her right shoulder. And there's no dispute that she has been diagnosed with a rotator cuff tear in her shoulder. But you're not going to hear undisputed evidence that happened in this accident.

During her deposition, Plaintiff testified that before this accident, she had NEVER had any right shoulder problems and hadn't had any treatment on her right shoulder before this accident. But the evidence is going to tell a different tale. The evidence is going to show that Plaintiff was involved in car wrecks in 2005, 2012, 2013, and 2014.

The evidence is going to show that from 2005 up to the time of this accident in February 2015, the Plaintiff treated at 5 different places for her shoulder. In February 2014, 1 year before this accident, she told her doctor she had constant pain in her shoulder for 7-8 years from falls and car wrecks.

The evidence is also going to show that 4 months after this wreck the Plaintiff had a fall where she hurt her right shoulder and went to the ER. And it wasn't until 1 month later that she got an MRI and was diagnosed with a rotator cuff tear.

Ladies and gentlemen, you have an important job. You have to listen to the evidence and decide which facts you believe are true. And as a part of that, you have to decide if the Plaintiff is trying to make my client pay for things that she didn't break.

There are other ways to prepare as well. One of my partners likes to make an outline and practice his delivery to several audiences — usually another lawyer, his staff, and his spouse. This allows him to work out all the kinks in his opening statement and get comfortable with what he wants to say.

As you might expect, lawyers feel strongly about opening statements. And for good reason. It's an important aspect of trial. Up next is a discussion among lawyers about the best methods of preparing for giving opening statements.

18

A DISCUSSION ABOUT PREPARING FOR OPENING STATEMENTS

I t can be difficult to get lawyers to provide not only war stories but also useful information and ideas about trial strategies, but that's what we have here. Lawyers from varying practice areas, locations, and experience levels having a conversation about the methods they use to prepare for giving opening statements at trial.

Alan: I've done it both ways, extemporaneous (from an outline) and written out.

Bret: I would write it out absolutely, but memorize it enough to where it appears extemporaneous.

Alan: I actually prefer the written out and memorized because it will change extemporaneously.

Bret: Shooting from the hip sounds like a very bad idea, even from a defense perspective, because of the possibility of being sidetracked by what the other guy said.

Joe: I always exert a level of prep for themes but never write it out. I'm big on improv. Even jury selection can impact the tenor of your opening, so I try to tailor to the jury in front of me.

Mark: Echo the above. I scribble an outline of an opening in the five minutes to an hour between jury selection and openings, just because writing helps me remember. But I don't take anything written up with me.

Nathan: For my bench trials (which tend to be auto and slip-and-fall defense), I don't write out an opening beyond some bullet points and base my response off of Plaintiff's opening. For larger civil trials I tend to have presentation/PowerPoint done with specific points, imaging, experts we might hear from, witnesses, etc. Nothing scripted but at least specific points. I do try to tailor emphasis of certain things or add/remove post jury selection based on how I think they will respond, however.

Joe: That's all great input. Because of that I also really don't emphasize my openings. Personally, I don't see as much value. My real value is first in jury selection. You're previewing issues with your people in a very real and personal way. I reference selection in my opening and closings. But opening is a rough preview of the evidence.

Robert: I'm in a different boat, as I've never given an opening. I have, however, seen them from a clerk's perspective and a paralegal in the gallery who had to watch the jurors. What I think works is simplicity and tone. There are times when you need the PowerPoint – everyone does them in asbestos because no one knows what it is. But you don't need to tell them everything up front. You just need to build investment and interest.

Kate: My trial experience is fairly limited since I'm still a baby lawyer - so far only bench trials and trial team. However, from that, here's my insight: I think notes are important but not to be glued to them. There's a fine balance between not memorizing the full open but not being glued to your notes the whole time (because you disconnect from the jury and cannot read/react to them).

Also, body language and positioning are very important from a human interest/psych perspective. Wandering around the room is distracting, but so is firmly planting and standing still (unless at a podium and even then, try to move a bit). I use my position for sign posts. Stand here whenever I talk about X event, stand there for Y event – it helps for people who are visual learners to make and keep the connection and remember the facts.

Adrian: I look at a trial like a filmmaker who was hired to write a screenplay based on a book. The opening statement is the most deliberate part of the whole trial. I can't imagine not writing it out. It does set the tone, but it also is about an introduction to the jury of your clients and their case. Presumably, you have already picked the "story" out that you want to tell. You can't gloss over the facts. You need to present the jury with something that will keep them engaged, but not stretch the truth. Kind, deliberate, and professional.

As you can see, every lawyer will approach preparing for opening statements a bit differently. No way is absolutely right (although there might be some ways that are definitely wrong). You have to figure out what works best for you and allows you to be most comfortable in front of the jury. And even after you have refined your processes, it is important to perform internal audits to make sure things are working as well as you think (and if not, not determine what changes to make).

19

SET THE TONE FOR TRIAL WITH YOUR OPENING STATEMENT

Your opening statement should set the tone for what the jury can expect from you for the rest of trial. Tone has several dimensions. Disposition – whether your presentation of the case will be aggressive or agreeable. Demeanor – are you affable and charming or all business? Delivery – whether you're engaging or monotonous. How I present my case and myself to the jury changes with each trial and depends on the facts and my arguments.

You read my bullet-pointed opening statement recently. That was a case in which the parties agreed about how the motorcycle wreck had happened. We agreed what the plaintiff's injuries were and which treatment related to the accident. We agreed about everything except how much the case was worth. And that is exactly what I had planned to tell the jury. My opening would be short to emphasize there wasn't much to this case. And I would be as agreeable as possible, because I was representing the insurance company, and that can be a hard chore.

War stories about setting the tone with your opening statement

Mark: Openings absolutely should set the tone for the rest of trial. Contrast my first trial with my last trial. In the first trial, a pathological liar tried to shoplift, then called her disbarred lawyer boyfriend to come help. He didn't tell anyone he wasn't her lawyer, then he gave her an incriminating piece of evidence which she folded up and shoved into her bra ... on video.

In the last trial, a career criminal got drunk and beat up his girlfriend, an older woman with terminal lung cancer. He left, and the upstairs neighbors came down to help her. He came back with a big knife. The upstairs neighbor tried to intervene, and he stabbed the neighbor in the chest.

One opening was very somber, leaning on calling this guy a hero, and asking what could have happened if he *hadn't* been there. The other opening was just playing the video and almost laughing ... because it was a ridiculous, dumb, almost fun trial, and nothing was at stake. There wasn't really a victim - only Kroger, who got their stuff back since they apprehended her in the store.

Robert: Tone matters *a lot*. The monotone guys who sit behind the podium lose jurors fast. The animated people who change up their speed and tone keep juror attention.

I did a lot of mock trial in law school and did very well at it, despite it being something I got little training in, and I really do believe in composure. I do practice a lot and am a big believer in theory and theme (actually, I'm a big believer in doing it throughout your case, not just at trial). But composure matters more than anything. We live in a society that watches *Law and Order*, *CSI*, and any number of bizarre legal shows where everyone is pithy. We aren't trained actors, but we are compared against them.

Nathan: To this point, I lost a he-said-she-said trial last year and the jury basically said I didn't put on enough of a dog-and-pony show whereas Plaintiff did.

Robert: I admire your restraint in not strangling them for saying that.

Nathan: They were sold by him really selling his client's story, even though it was somewhat incredulous, and my taking what I perceived as the more reasonable road of just clarifying things. It was tough because they were essentially saying that had I been more animated and seemed "more convincing" somehow, they might have been swayed to my side, which I think was objectively more reasonable.

That's a tough proposition for me because I know my cases inside and out and present them based on facts, logic, etc. But I think they were basically saying, you didn't have that 'you can't handle the truth' moment that made us believe in the case so that's why you lost. Time to sign up for acting lessons I suppose

Robert: I think that can also just be them saying that they didn't believe that you believed your story. You were reasonable, but you didn't live it like the other guy did.

Nathan: That could also be true. The whole thing was just crazy and stupid. Essentially, a verbal altercation between the aunt and baby-momma resulting in an alleged hit-and-run (and this is a civil lawsuit). People were throwing bleach at each other! The one woman is supposedly thrown onto the hood and carried for a block to be thrown off. The Plaintiff couldn't produce her witnesses. Everything about her story reeked of fabrication. And my lady was just like "Yeah, that's nuts. It didn't happen." So I went with the "[Eyeroll] This lady is out to get her and this seems fabricated" story.

Robert: Oof.

Nathan: But that being said, it was a good point to have to internalize – trying harder to sell it without making it seem forced.

Those stories show the importance of setting the tone for trial with your opening statement. But they also show that you may have the facts and law on your side, but if you don't hit all the right notes the jury wants to hear, they might not go with you regardless.

20

USING YOUR OPENING STATEMENT AS A ROADMAP FOR TRIAL

Once upon a time, if you needed to get from Houston to Chattanooga, you would get out your trusty Rand McNally and plot your course. Using various waypoints, you'd figure out how to get from your launch point to your destination. An opening statement should be used in just the same way.

It should be a roadmap for the jury that gets them from the launch point (e.g., they've been seated on the jury panel and know nothing about the case) to the destination (e.g., entering a favorable verdict). The waypoints are the evidence you will reveal along the way that guides the jury and affirms to them they are on course.

One of the best ways to do this is with a theme you can emphasize throughout the case. A theme does not have to be a gimmicky catchphrase or tagline. But it should be something that binds together the story you're telling and the evidence you're presenting to support your case. You should lay the foundation for your theme during voir dire and use your opening to map out your case for the jury by showing how the facts align with your theory of the case.

Here are some thoughts on this topic from litigators in the legal community LawyerSmack.

Mark: I don't like rote "themes" - like, those catchy phrases that you repeat a few times throughout the trial. To me, they make you seem fake. *Too* practiced.

Nathan: I would say I just try to flesh out overarching themes as opposed to getting too specific for a variety of reasons, including because I don't want to say a jury will hear something and then due to evidentiary or other issues.

Kate: Themes are good. Trial is inherently boring, especially civil trials. I think a theme helps the jury stay engaged to an extent. If you can weave your theme through each phase of trial, it helps your points stick in jurors' minds. Themes are tough - you don't want to be cheesy. If the jury feels like you're trying to sell them, it will turn some people off to you. Content? Give them the 30,000 foot view of your case and then highlights of what you know you can/will prove. This gives them signposts to look forward to.

Also, general overarching concept for opening: juries inherently have a variety of different learning styles. One person learns best by listening, another by writing/engaging, another visually, etc. Understanding the way humans learn/internalize information and finding a style that subtly caters to all at once is very effective for not "losing" any of your jurors.

Alan: It is the roadmap for trial. At least from the plaintiff's perspective. I would assume it's the same from the defense side as well

Bret: If it doesn't set the theme, it's wasted.

Alan: Unless your defending a small car wreck and the plaintiff's lawyer gets up and gives an hour long opening and bores the s*** out of the jury. Then stand up and say something to the effect of "I don't want to waste your time listening to me. Let's just see what the evidence is and then let you decide."

Bret: Yeah, but that is somewhat risky. You better be *really sure* that they bored the jury. In closing, it could be argued, "They couldn't be bothered to tell you what they thought the evidence would show, because they know they can't argue with what the facts in this case are. I told you what it was, and they said, 'Ok, we'll see.' Well, guess what? You saw what the evidence says."

Alan: That also assumes the jury can disregard the "always about me" mentality. I would say in response to that, "We are here because we have been arguing about the facts for over 2 years of litigation. What I argue to you doesn't matter. What matters is the evidence presented to you. And there was no evidence of X."

Bret: I sure wouldn't say "what I argue to you doesn't matter." Haha. But yeah, focusing on the evidence is key.

When you are preparing for your opening statement, make sure to give thought to how you can use it as a roadmap to lead the jury to the destination you'd like them to arrive at - a favorable verdict.

21

CAN YOUR OPENING STATEMENT BE
USED AGAINST YOU?

A few years ago in a small county in eastern Alabama where there lies a notorious stock car superspeedway, we were trying a case. Our truck driver had been traveling behind a school bus, when the bus stopped at a set of railroad tracks. Our driver also stopped. The bus started forward again, then immediately stopped at a second set of railroad tracks. The truck driver did not stop this time. He had forgotten about the second set of tracks.

Several years later, some of the children riding the bus sued the driver and trucking company. We did discovery, took depositions, and ultimately concluded the children's claims for injuries were baseless. Even so, there is always some risk at trial, so our client made some settlement offers. We were never able to reach an agreement, so the parties prepared for trial.

After we selected the jury, I was tasked with delivering our opening statement. We were taking the somewhat risky position that neither were we negligent, nor were any of the kids hurt. There were several ways this could go wrong if the jury didn't buy our arguments.

A Clever Opening Statement

I needed to convince the jury our driver had not breached a duty, but he had competing duties — he had a duty to keep a proper lookout for other vehicles on the roadway, but he also had a duty to make sure his tractor and 53-foot trailer cleared the railroad tracks because it is illegal for a tractor-trailer to stop on the tracks. I had noticed our courtroom had markers on the walls denoting every ten feet starting at the back of the courtroom.

During my opening statement, I walked to the back of the courtroom. I then began walking slowly toward the jury telling them as I went all the things our driver had a duty to do and was doing as he started moving from his stopped position at the railroad tracks. He was checking his instrument clusters, watching the tracks in both directions for oncoming trains, using his mirror to determine whether he had cleared the tracks. It seemed pretty convincing, and I felt like it was a clever illustration. Until closing arguments.

During his closing argument, opposing counsel walked off that same distance to show how much time and distance the truck driver had to notice the big yellow school bus stopped in front of him. This also seemed to be convincing. I realized then I needed to consider more thoroughly how my opening statement may be used against me at other points of trial.

Make sure to deliver on evidence you promise

I was talking with another lawyer about opening statements, and here's what he had to say on the topic:

> Opening statements can definitely come back to bite you, in a couple of ways. One is if you go first — plaintiff or prosecutor (in Kentucky, anyway) — because the other side has the

benefit of hearing yours, and a savvy opposing counsel can turn your words against you or counter what you say. The other is if something you promise in your opening statements doesn't actually happen in trial — because of unexpected changing testimony, or an adverse ruling, or whatever. Then, opposing counsel can beat you up on it in closing — "Remember this morning, when the prosecution promised you that you'd hear from X? But you didn't, did you? Why do you think that is?"

Here are a couple of things to consider when crafting your opening statement to make sure that it doesn't come back to bite you: (1) do not promise evidence you can't deliver, and (2) there is a flip side to almost every illustration. Scrutinize what you say in your opening statement to make sure it provides a roadmap for the jury, gives them a compelling story, and does not give ammunition to your opponent.

22

SHOULD YOU ASK JUDGES IF THEY ARE FAMILIAR WITH YOUR CASE?

I n a conversation about oral arguments, this question came up: What is the most polite way to ask judges whether they are familiar with the briefs or would they prefer if I summarize the facts and issues for them?[1]

I wasn't going to pretend to know the answer. I've argued my share of motions with varying degrees of success, but oral arguments are not my strong suit. So I put my historian hat back on and decided to go find some primary sources to answer the question.

There is no more readily accessible place to find judges and experienced lawyers willing to share their wisdom and preferences than Twitter, which is exactly where I went to find the answer to the question of whether to assume the judge you're arguing before knows the facts of your case.

Responses from appellate and trial judges

Chief Judge Stephen Dillard (@JudgeDillard) of the Georgia Court of Appeals: "You should presume that the judge (or judges) have read your brief. If you aren't asked any questions out of the gate, quickly frame the issue and then lead with your strongest argument. If it's a cold bench, make your key points and sit down." Justice Jerod Tufte (@JudgeTufte) of the North Dakota Supreme Court replied: "Tufte, J., concurring emphatically."

Justice Beth Walker (@bethwalkr) of the West Virginia Supreme Court of Appeals: "We routinely instruct lawyers (politely) during oral arguments to focus on the legal issue(s) and assume we are familiar with the facts. Because we are." Justice Rhonda Wood (@JudgeRhondaWood) of the Arkansas Supreme Court agreed: "That is right! If you are spending time on the facts, you are 9/10 wasting valuable time."

Alabama Circuit Court Judge John H. Graham (@Legal-Moonshiner): "If it's the first time there's been a hearing on this particular case, counsel must assume the judge is fact-ignorant. But if it's been there before, plow on into the law. The judge will tell you if she or he doesn't remember the facts. And don't forget that we have many, many cases, some with similar facts and names alike. I have, for instance, 1,497 active cases across 3 divisions ... plus drug court. Sometimes it all runs together."

Alabama Circuit Court Judge Jenifer Collins Holt (@Jenifer-Holt): "First, if the brief is lengthy, I recommend that you send a paper copy. Second, I prefer a summary in either event so no need to ask. Seeing and hearing the attorneys gives me a better feel for the dynamics of the case. If it's a motion to reconsider, disregard both. :grinning:"

Responses among the litigators

Jason Thompson (@jrt219) of Grayling, Michigan: "Start with your timed, uninterrupted presentation ready. If they're silent that's relatively thorough with the facts, which is kind of their cue to move to questioning if they want to. If not, stay the course. And the way I would frame your question about facts is to always assume they've read it but may not recall each pertinent fact. So if it comes up on an issue, you're asking if they want you to review the facts with them 'again.'"

Jason Steed (@5thCircAppeals) of Forma Legalis, Dallas: "In my oral argument last week I started to answer a question about waiver by saying, 'To help the court understand what happened ...' and the judge said, 'The court understands the case, Counsel.' (ouch)"

Raffi Melkonian (@RMFifthCircuit) of Wright, Close & Barger in Houston: "Yep. Smack, smack, smack. I will sometimes say, 'Let me give you some background that I think is important to answer that question' or a similar thing, if I think there's a factual misunderstanding."

Travis Ramey (@bamalaw2011) of Birmingham, Alabama: "I've tried something similar to that and gotten: 'What I'd like you to give me is an answer to my question.' If the court decides it needs to hit you, it will. All you can do is roll with the hits, keep answering questions, and look for pivot points."

Stacy Moon (@StacyMoon02), of F&B Law Firm, Huntsville, Alabama: "'Your honor, would you like me to remind you of the facts at issue, or do you prefer we focus solely on the legal argument?' just start with the facts, and let the judge interrupt and move you on."

If the judges and justices above didn't make it clear, you have a limited time in front of your audience, so there's something to be said for brevity. Here's an example from the justice editor at ThinkProgress news website, Ian Millhiser (@imillhiser): "The best oral argument I've seen was 'This case is before you on an abuse of discretion standard. Unless you think the district judge abused his discretion by finding that firing a gun into a building is dangerous, you must affirm. Unless there are questions, I'll take my seat.'"

Parsing the Results

Courts have heavy caseloads. Trial courts have a tremendous number of cases they're dealing with and typically, many cases they are hearing in a single sitting or motion docket. While the trial court may have read your brief and be somewhat familiar with your case, judges Graham's and Holt's responses suggest you may be best served by briefly reciting the facts of the case for their benefit before launching into your argument.

Appellate courts, on the other hand, have the luxury of selecting the cases they'll hear on oral arguments and decide. With a lighter caseload, appellate judges have more time to spend with each case before hearing it. The responses above reveal a uniform desire among them for lawyers to dive right into the legal issues.

When deciding how best to approach on oral arguments, know your audience and rely on your experience and training. If you don't have experience in front of a particular judge, poll other lawyers in your office or community of lawyers. Be mindful that regardless of anyone else's experience or their shared wisdom, your mileage may vary.

23
_____

CHOOSING MONEY OVER INTEGRITY

I ntegrity is hard. It requires diligence and guardianship. Integrity is a fragile thing that can be shattered like a candle globe. Once broken, even if reassembled, others are not going to have the same trust in it being structurally sound as they had before.

Integrity in the face of a client's dishonesty

During some settlement discussions about a case pending in one of the more liberal venues in Alabama, opposing counsel and I were talking about the merits of the case to try to reach a settlement agreement. He pointed out the liability for the accident — there was no disputing that. His client had incurred some medical expenses and undergone not insignificant treatment. Because of these things and the venue, he was making a policy limits demand.

It was my turn to present my side. As the uninsured motorist carrier, I didn't have any motivation to offer my policy limits – even on my worst day (which might be bad in that county), my client couldn't lose any more than it was contractually obligated to pay. But more importantly, the plaintiff had outright lied in her deposition about some things. Important things. Things about her pre-existing condition, past medical treatment, and prior lawsuits. And we had wrapped all those lies into a nice, tidy undeniable package.

When I mentioned the problems with the plaintiff's testimony to opposing counsel, he didn't say, "Yeah, I understand that's going to be a problem I'll have to deal with." He didn't say, "I think I can still rehabilitate my client afterward." There were any number of responses that would have been appropriate. I've been on both sides of this conversation before, both bearing witness to the lying and having the client who lied. I know what the usual responses are.

I did not get the response I expected. What opposing counsel said was, "Eh. We'll just tell the jury she's old and forgot about it." [Just for context here, we're talking about her *forgetting* about years of prior problems with this part of her body, a workers' compensation claim, and a lawsuit]. "Besides," he added, "the jury won't like you if you beat her up about it. So..."

I was impressed. I wasn't looking for him to be contrite on behalf of his client. But neither was I expecting him to be dismissive of her dishonesty because ... venue.

There were many things I was inclined to say in response. None of them were kind. But none of them needed to be said. Now I know where he's going to land on these kinds of issues in the future, and that's enough.

What I said was, "Okay. Well, I've made my offer, and it's never going to be higher than that."

He replied, "I think the jury is going to give my client more than your policy limits."

"Maybe. We'll take that chance."

The fallout of choosing temporal things

You can't make your client's decisions for them. If they choose
to lie during a deposition, you have some options. You can just
let them be dishonest, hoping that opposing counsel is not
aware of their misappropriation of the facts. You could pause
the deposition, step out with your client, then come back in to
"clarify" something. Or if you are unaware of the lies at the time
of their occurrence (which sometimes happens because — and
you may find this hard to believe — some clients aren't forth-
right with their own lawyers), you can try to fix them later by
amending responses to Interrogatories. Or at the very least, you
can acknowledge the problem during conversations with
opposing counsel.

But if you choose otherwise, if you choose to stand behind
your client's lies rather than to remediate them, you're going to
burn bridges with opposing counsel. The next time I'm
tempted to make a small misrepresentation or be outright
dishonest, I'm going to try to keep this in mind — whatever the
matter at hand, it is not worth shattering my integrity with the
other person. If she can't trust me to be honest, we can't have a
working relationship, which will make the next thirty years of
practicing law harder than necessary.

24

USING AUTO-CORRECT SETTINGS AS A
PREVENTATIVE MEASURE

T here are some words and acronyms that are difficult to remember how to spell correctly. For example, I have to consciously think about how to spell marriage. That "ia" is always trying to trip me up. There are other words too, some more commonly misspelled than others. Then there are words that my fingers just type out-of-order when I'm trying to fly through a brief. But you can minimize those mistakes and make your life easier by using auto-correct settings to fix your common problems.

Recognizing Your Mistakes

Perhaps one of the most avoidable mistakes I see made by lawyers and paralegals is misspelling the acronym for the Health Information Portability and Accountability Act (HIPAA). Too commonly, I see it written as HIPPA, and sometimes I see it both ways within the same document; below is a real-life example:

<u>Motion for HIPPA Order</u>

COMES NOW the Defendant, by and through the undersigned counsel of record, and respectfully requests that this Honorable Court issue an order requiring all health care providers, health plan administrators and other individuals who may be in possession of health information that is protected by the privacy regulations issued pursuant to the Health Insurance Portability and Accessibility Act of 1996 (HIPAA), to produce said information.

I tweeted about this specific problem a while ago. The responses I received from a half dozen folks confirmed that I am not the only person seeing this. In fact, some people are insistently incorrect. Scott Hunter (@SWHesq) replied. "I've had folks try and tell me my release is insufficient (I spent a day going through the CFRs when I was a baby lawyer – I know it's right). Almost always the person complaining would spell it HIPPA."

The trouble is people are not recognizing their mistake, even though if they read the name of the statute, it would be readily apparent to them. But other common mistakes can be easily resolved if the user is willing to set up some auto-correct features.

Using auto-correct settings

Whether you use Microsoft Word or Word Perfect (because there are an inordinate number of lawyers out there still using Word Perfect), you can use auto-correct settings to help resolve spelling mistakes you commonly make. Here are some step-by-step instructions for adjusting your auto-correct settings to be useful for you.

If you use one of the more recent iterations of Microsoft Word, go to the File menu and drop all the way down to

Options. You will need to click on the Proofing menu, which will bring up the following screen.

When you click on AutoCorrect Options, you will see in the middle of the pop-up box an option to "Replace" any word of your choosing "With" any other word. I recommend replacing HIPPA with HIPAA. After typing in your selection and clicking the "Add" button, Word will automatically correct the mistake for you going forward.

Of course if your practice is anything like mine and you're dealing with bodily injuries and anatomical parts all day, you have bigger problems than HIPAA. You are running into words like "spondylolisthesis" and Word places one of those scraggly red lines under it because it doesn't recognize the word. There is a solution for you here too.

Adding words to your dictionary

There are a couple of ways to add words to your dictionary in Word. The easiest is to right-click on the purportedly misspelled word. Follow the arrow to the right of "Spelling" and click on "Add to Dictionary." And you're done. The red line will disappear from under the word. You may need to do this for both capitalized and non-capitalized versions of the word.

Ever since I started regularly using a computer (way back even before days of Windows 3.1), I have looked for and used shortcuts that make my workflow easier. You ought to be using technology to make your life and your practice easier because it is important that to stay ahead of the competition you are the most efficient and effective version of yourself. One of the most productive ways to do that is to exploit the features of software you are already running to eliminate common and unnecessary mistakes.

PART III

PRACTICE MANAGEMENT

25

TWO DISTINCTIONS BETWEEN GOOD LAWYERS AND BAD LAWYERS

I would rather deal with a good lawyer than a bad lawyer every single time. Even a lawyer who is more experienced or who I perceive as better than me. I don't think I have a particularly high bar in what I want from opposing counsel. In fact I can break it down into two easy categories: (1) know how to evaluate and handle your cases, and (2) don't be a lying liar who lies. On days when I start to get greedy, I also want an opposing counsel who's easy to get along with, but I can at least be satiated if they meet the first two criteria.

Good Lawyers Know How to Evaluate and Handle Cases

By and large, knowing how to handle cases is not too difficult, but it does take some experience. This isn't to say that everyone handles their cases appropriately. There are plenty of lawyers who, after suing, go dark. They refuse to respond to phone calls and emails from opposing counsel, or even their clients. They can't be bothered to respond to discovery until a court compels them to do so. In short, they are lazy or indifferent — qualities that make for bad lawyers.

There is also a matter of knowing how to evaluate your cases. Settlement can be hard enough as is, but when a lawyer doesn't know what his case is worth and doesn't know how to properly evaluate it, settlement can be all but impossible. Several years ago, I was assigned a new case. I opened the file to find that my clients were roofers who had been re-tarring an elementary school gymnasium. Unbeknown to them, there was a small hole in the roof that allowed some of the hot tar to slip through and down onto a student inside the gym. When I saw those facts and the plaintiff's $200,000 demand, I thought we were in for a rough ride. Then I saw the photographs.

The photographs showed a nickel-sized injury on the plaintiff's upper arm. I had been envisioning massive burns and scarring. This case was pending in the most conservative venue in the state. It immediately became clear that I was dealing with a lawyer who was out of his depth. He didn't know where he was or what his case was worth. It took us a while to get the case positioned for a reasonable settlement. My opponent's inexperience cost me time and my client money, in a way that wouldn't have been necessary if he had known how to evaluate his case.

I am not suggesting that even when there are two experienced lawyers working a case they will evaluate the matter similarly. There are many times when my opponent and I evaluate cases differently, but I know how they arrived at their evaluation. I expect that to happen. We have different goals. I am not assuming every time a plaintiff wants more for their injury than my client is willing to give that they don't know what they're doing. The difference is we can each explain how we arrived at our evaluations.

Lying Liars Who Lie Are Inherently Bad Lawyers

If you've spent any time watching the USA show *Suits* about a bunch of BigLaw guys in New York, then you've seen the worst (or best?) examples of what I'm talking about here. Every relationship is adversarial and everyone is trying to get an edge over one another through deception and trickeration. You have only to look at the two protagonists to reach this conclusion: Harvey Specter is a beguiling litigator who has quickly risen to the top of the food-chain because he's ruthless (and devilishly handsome), and Mike Ross is a genius con-man who purported to be a Harvard-educated lawyer. Here's the thing about those guys: the lawyers in their own firm can't trust them; opposing counsel can't trust them; and often, their own clients can't trust them. This sort of behavior makes for bad lawyers.

In contrast, a friend of mine recently confessed, "I was one of those crappy lawyers today." He was working on two similar cases in which he had received settlement offers. In telling his clients about the offers, he had gotten mixed up and told Client A about Offer B and vice versa. The clients declined the offers, so my friend sent out denial letters, explaining the basis for the denials and fired off some discovery. Opposing counsel was at a loss trying to understand the explanations that didn't match facts of the cases.

In discovering his error, my friend could have gotten defensive and tried to cover his tracks ... but that is what a crappy lawyer would have done. Instead, he sent out an apology letter right away, explaining what had happened. He also immediately informed the clients about the screw-up. The clients still rejected the offers on their respective cases. And my friend maintained his integrity by owning up to his mistake: "That's just how I live life. I'm not going to hide things or blame other people. Always easier in life to face the consequences now, before they grow."

In a burst of frustration, another lawyer in this same conversation described bad lawyers as the ones "who misrepresent material facts — don't consult their clients before making allegations - who file seemingly deliberately shoddy pleadings and ignore court orders and rules to try to squirrel away some kind of marginal advantage — whom an outsider might at first mistake for a pro se litigant." Mix-ups happen. Mistakes happen. Screw-ups don't make for bad lawyers. Lying about and covering up screw-ups makes for bad lawyers.

In preparing a case for trial, I discovered I had inadvertently disclosed something to opposing counsel that, if she realized it, could harm my case. I realized this about 10:00pm a few days before our pretrial conference. I tossed and turned all night thinking about how to tell my partner about my screw-up. Now, it was probable that opposing counsel wouldn't discover my disclosure, so it was also probable my partner would never know about it, unless I told him. I could have just waited things out to see how they developed. But I didn't. First thing the next morning, I stepped into my partner's office and let him know. As it turned out, opposing counsel never realized my mistake (or at least, never let on if she had). My partner never would have known if I hadn't self-reported. But I would have fretted over it for two weeks. And I would have known I was being disingenuous with someone I trust and who trusts me.

If you aspire to be a good lawyer, here are two criteria to consider: (1) do you know how to manage and evaluate your cases — and if not, are you actively pursuing improvement; and (2) can the people you regularly interact with trust you? If the answer to either of those questions is no, you've got some work to do. If the answer is yes, then you've still got to work to maintain your positions. And sometimes maintaining a practice and reputation are harder than building it in the first place.

26

HAVE SOMETHING TO SAY BUT NOT SURE YOU'RE QUALIFIED?

W hen I started my law blog in June 2016, I did so without too much trepidation.[1] I was essentially briefing cases and writing about my practice in ways that I was pretty comfortable with. After a few months, I wanted to branch out. I started to have ideas about things I would like to write about other than recent appellate decisions. That's where things started to feel dicey. I wasn't sure I was qualified to write about these other things.

I started slowly. After reading, Stephen King's *On Writing*, I wrote a (mostly derivative) post about how writing like Stephen King would improve your legal writing. When that went fine, a month later I wrote a personal piece about learning some hard lessons about failure from a bad experience with a rental property. A few days after posting the article about failure, I got an email from a lawyer I knew who was going through the same thing and was appreciative to have someone to commiserate with.

With the confidence I developed from those experiences, I branched out into writing about client management. And this was where I really had concerns about how others would perceive my qualifications. I was a fourth-year associate writing about maintaining and developing relationships with clients. What could I tell lawyers who had been practicing far longer? At that time, I wasn't sure.

But I had something to say. I was interested in my topic, had talked to people about it, read about it, ruminated on it, and practiced what I was writing about. I felt that what I had to say about the metrics that corporate clients use to measure the performance of outside counsel was well-founded and could help both attorneys and their clients. I was compelled to write about it despite what, on paper, looked like limited qualifications.

That post about client metrics, which I published in December 2016, set the tone for the three areas I now write about the most and which this book is about: case management, client management, and practice management. That is the content that helped my blog grow, evolved into my first book, *Building a Better Law Practice*, and eventually into this second book. If I hadn't taken a step off that precipitous ledge, many opportunities that are before me now would not have developed.

So when a friend of mine, RI Smith, mentioned the other day that what was holding him back from launching his website was concern about whether he was credentialed enough to opine about legal writing, I told him to take the plunge:

RIS: My problem is that I have two types of issues — legal curiosities that take a long time to digest to my satisfaction and tearing apart/fawning over well written pleadings and opinions. I'm qualified to do the first, but shy away from the latter, outside of LawyerSmack. What I like and what others like are different things.

JWR: You shouldn't shy from it. You're plenty smart enough to have/share your opinion publicly about it.

RIS: Well, it's the difference between, "I clerked and read hundreds of motions and memos and this is what I thought was most convincing," and "You shouldn't do these things."

JWR: Support your argument, and if people disagree, then fine. They'll go on writing their briefs the same way it's been done for 40 years.

RIS: Yeah, which is fine. It's a longer version of Judge Kozinski's video about not boring him. Write your own stuff, don't cite long passages of law. Give me the good stuff. We just have different views on what the good stuff is. And I am probably the oddity that reads nearly every single page of exhibits which were submitted.

JWR: There's definitely a market for those ideas. Look what Bryan Garner and Ross Guberman have been able to do for themselves.

RIS: Well, Ross is why I say I'm not qualified. I've been tearing apart my style based upon his work.

JWR: Ross started somewhere too.

RIS: That's true.

JWR: Just because he's uber-qualified doesn't mean you're not qualified, even if you disagree with him.

RIS: Sure. I think it's just been more finding where I am qualified and hitting on those points.

JWR: I'm a sixth-year associate writing about client management and case management. There are people on my email list who've been practicing for 5x as long. It can be intimidating. But you can't let that hinder you.

RIS: Well, it helps that you're good at that. Thanks for the advice. It's something I've been putting off because I'm consistently sure I'm not qualified to say anything except to someone asking me.

JWR: To the extent that I'm any good at it, it's because I care about it, read about it, and think a lot about it. Which sounds like the same way you are with the legal writing stuff. Come on in, the water's fine.

I would say the same thing to any lawyer who is considering branching out into something they are unsure they will be seen as qualified for. If you educate yourself about your subject. If it's something you care about. If it's something you feel compelled to write articles or blog entries, record YouTube videos, or publish podcasts about, then just do it.

You may make missteps along the way. I have. You may shout into the void for a while before you find both your voice and your audience. I did. But here's something I firmly believe: there is no more certain way to learn and grow than to put yourself in the precarious position of failing, especially when you might fail publicly.

27

WHAT DO ASSOCIATES WANT FROM THEIR FIRMS?

The associates you hire want to do a good job. They strive to become good lawyers.[1] They recognize the demands that are placed on them for their time, attention, and skills. They are up for the challenge, but they need some help along the way.

There are things firms and partners can do to make a work environment and career trajectory more tenable. But not just *tenable*, which seems like a minimum threshold. Rather, there are affirmative things you can do to help your associates thrive and succeed in a way that promotes growth, strengthens the firm, and encourages loyalty.

What struggles are associates experiencing?

The associates you hire are under a tremendous amount of strain — things they try not to exhibit in the office because they know it's their problem and not yours. It affects them nonetheless.

Financial Burdens. Financial burdens: As tuition and associated law school costs continue to soar, many young associates are graduating law school with a financial burden of student loans not seen by previous generations. According to "Law School Transparency," a February 1, 2018 ABA Journal article by Stephanie Francis Ward, recent law grads had on average $134,497 in law school debt if they went to a private school or $96,054 in law school debt if they went to a public school.

While the job market has recovered somewhat from the lowest ebb earlier this decade, it is still a grim place for new graduates. According to ABA data in a May 11, 2017 ABAJournal.com post by Ward, out of 37,124 people who graduated in 2016 from ABA-accredited law schools, nearly 73 percent had full-time long-term jobs requiring or preferring a JD. And because fewer students were attending law school, that figure represented a 4.1 percent decline in such jobs from 2015. Those who have been hired are likely earning less than they had expected going into law school. Their monthly student loan payments are the size of mortgages and eat up a considerable percentage of their net income.

These financial burdens bring pressure that is always lurking, waiting for an opportunity to create anxiety.

Difficult Work Environments. A hostile work atmosphere in which everyone is only seeking his own best interests can quickly become toxic. An office doesn't have to be a place where everyone gets to work with their best friends, but it does need to be a place where there are people with amicable and supportive relationships.

Is your firm cultivating a collection of people who are willing to go out of their way to help one another out? This can be done in part by hiring people for qualities over skills, and more importantly, by those in leadership positions exhibiting a spirit of cooperation and collaboration, not only to those who are on a lateral plane but also to their subordinates.

Imposter Syndrome. When new associates enter a firm, they often hear, "Fake it 'til you make it." Unwittingly, they have entered a world for which law school has only minimally prepared them. Some will land at supportive firms, where a partner or another associate is able and willing to guide them. Others will be left to flounder. Some will have the vision and assertiveness to set goals for themselves for self-evaluation and development. More will not. Young associates need guidance and structure that will help them get their bearings as they learn to practice law.

What are associates looking for from their firms?

As with any relationship in which there is a power imbalance, there is often a lack of effective communication between partners and associates. It is not usually intentional and even less often is it insidious. But typically, neither side is open-mindedly asking the other what is important to them. Here are some things that are important to associates as they consider their futures at a firm and look to advance.

Opportunity. Opportunity takes many forms. It is something associates crave from their firms. Opportunities to grow in their practice areas, opportunities to try practice areas of greater interest to them, opportunities to lead, and opportunities to advance. One Georgia lawyer was looking for "opportunities to specialize in practice areas we find interesting. Advancement talks are too focused on the associate-to-partner track. That's not the only means of advancement."

An associate in Pennsylvania is looking for the opportunity to lead: "There should be opportunities for non-partners to take on additional responsibility, and be afforded increased compensation, for instance, by taking on a 'team leader' type role in a practice group. Or by spear-heading a new branch of business under a partner's supervision. I might not be ready to be a partner in 3-5 years, but if there are newer associates that come in during that time, being able to take a team leadership type role would be something I'd be interested in, particularly if it came with some perks/additional pay. Plus, it might be a good way to groom associates for partner by allowing them to lead without having to be rainmakers at the same time."

A California insurance defense associate had two thoughts about what opportunity looked like for her: "Opportunity is important. If you're not given increasingly greater responsibility, challenges, and chances to do all aspects of a case (*e.g.*, mediation, arguing motions, and trial), then an associate will look elsewhere to get those things." As with many associates, she expressed that there had not been communication about a "clear path to advancement. So often it's all smoke and mirrors about what it takes to make partner. I know I need to land a client and bring in money. But how much and for how long?" This was mirrored by an associate at an insurance defense firm in Mississippi: "Firms should try to do a better job at selling to younger attorneys that sticking with them and trying to advance is a good investment career-wise for the attorney. This would require firms to pull back the curtains a bit, which many firms seem to not be thrilled with doing."

These associates are all looking to improve themselves and their practices. They are looking for their firms to give them a reason to stick around and help the firm grow along with them. Partners can provide the guidance associates need to accomplish their goals when they are aware of the opportunities their associates are seeking to develop, lead, and advance.

Direction. A Michigan patent attorney told me that he was looking at his firm to provide "a somewhat clear path. Having the end in sight, however far away, is good motivation and helps us figure out if we're progressing."

To thrive, young lawyers need structure and support. A mentor who has a vested interest in their development and success and with whom they can openly discuss concerns. They need feedback on the work they're performing — instruction, reinforcement, and criticism. This level of development aids in laying the foundation for a successful professional career. The early years of practice will effectively mold the lawyer into the practitioner she will be for the next forty years. When you provide effective feedback, it is timely and specific. The U.S. Office of Personnel Management has given the following advice.[2] Regarding timeliness, "Employees should receive information about how they're doing as timely as possible. If improvement needs to be made in their performance, the sooner they find out about it the sooner they can correct the problem. If employees have reached or exceeded a goal, the sooner they receive positive feedback, the more rewarding it is to them." As for specificity, "Telling employees that they are doing well because they exceeded their goal by 10% is more effective than simply saying, 'You're doing a good job.'"

Your associates need to know how they are measuring up. They need to hear from you whether they're meeting expectations and what they can do to improve. If you want to put them in the best position to succeed, your associates need specific, measurable goals that will create the opportunity for you to give specific performance feedback.

Stability. By a wide margin, the strongest responses when I asked associates what they are looking for from their firms was *stability*. When lawyers feel secure in their jobs, they are more inclined to be emotionally invested in their work and loyal toward their employers. I have had the great fortune to be at the same firm since I started practicing. My firm has had a consistent leadership structure throughout that time and has provided a stable foundation for my development. But the responses I received from other associates have me believing I may be among the minority.

An associate at a Virginia firm was looking for stability and some sense of responsibility out of the partners: "My firm is in a constant state of chaos because the partners can't seem to coordinate or sit still long enough to get things done, or come up with a plan for how to handle some of our recurring issues. At this point, if they asked me if I wanted a promotion with a raise, I'd refuse, because I don't want to be at all responsible for when the firm eventually fails." A general practitioner in Canada remarked that he was seeking "stability and good leadership/management. No sense in advancing into a dysfunctional environment."

A lawyer secure in her environment and with stability around her will be comfortable shouldering more responsibility and taking measured risks. She will know that a mistake won't necessarily result in a job loss, but an opportunity to grow. She will be in an environment where she can grow intellectually and professionally. This lawyer will have a secure platform from which she can build a successful practice.

Providing for the Needs of Your Associates Strengthens the Firm

There are plenty of "average" lawyers who are practicing law. Keith Lee of LawyerSmack is wont to say, "The average lawyer isn't very good ... and fifty percent are worse than that." We don't need more of those lawyers. Rather, we need lawyers who have been put in positions to thrive, for whom others have put in the time, energy, and devotion to help them stretch their intellectual limits, have critiqued them to higher performance levels, and generally prodded them to caring and achieving more than the "average" lawyer. We need lawyers who are at their best.

By recognizing the needs of their associates, firms can enable their young lawyers to achieve more. It takes consistency, commitment, and intentionality to create an environment in which lawyers can not merely survive, but thrive. By serving its young lawyers, the partners are serving themselves and strengthening their firms.

28

PREPARING FOR THE TRANSITION FROM ASSOCIATE TO PARTNER

W hat makes for a good associate is not necessarily what makes for a good partner. The two have very different roles in a firm. A good associate works diligently, knows the expectations his partners have of him, and fully immerses himself in his practice areas so he can meet his clients' needs. But these things alone do not prepare an associate for a partnership, which is presumably where most associates would like to end up.

The trouble is most associates receive little guidance on what partners are looking for to enable associates not only to receive a partnership offer but also to make a successful transition. To help fill that gap, I interviewed four lawyers: Stacy Moon of F&B Law Firm in Huntsville, AL; Francisco Ramos of Clark Silvergate in Miami, FL; Danielle Dietrich of Tucker Arensburg in Pittsburgh, PA; and a partner at a mid-sized regional firm who wished to remain anonymous.

What characteristics or qualities make for a good associate?

SM: Curiosity — wanting to know why a court made a ruling in a case; wanting to understand how decisions are made or how a case assessment was reached. Thinking outside the box — when given a form or "go by," having the courage to make changes to the language because it seems too formalistic and not sufficiently clear; considering ways out of a suit (or additional claims against a party) that might not be included in the "last" pleading. Understanding that a law school degree does not mean that person automatically knows everything. Being detail oriented and an excellent writer.

FR: Strong work ethic, 24/7 availability, and imagination.

DD: Good listening skills, awareness of your role, doing things when you say you will, and update shareholders on progress.

AN: My firm tends to staff leanly (often only one associate per matter), so we look for smart self-starters with good people skills (as they often have early client contact) who can think on their feet and hit the ground running. Our litigation associates, for example, handle depositions, court hearings, and have client interaction fairly early on in their tenure at the firm.

What helps you identify whether an associate is ready to become a partner?

SM: Frequently, the questions an associate asks are indicators. Are they more thought process questions or basic? Is the associate taking an interest in developing business, not just practicing law? Is the associate looking for ways to get his or her name out, as well as the firm's? In crunch times, is the associate okay with working extra hours? [In turn, in our office, in slower work periods, we understand taking advantage of those times to take care of other items.]

Is the associate demonstrating that he or she is considering the firm as a whole, not just the "work"? The biggest attitude change between an associate and a partner is the reaction to closing the firm for weather. While I always appreciate a snow day (and I love snow), my other thought is almost always how much are we going to lose in billables that day.

FR: Their efforts to do more than just billable work.

DD: When you don't worry about all of those things that make for a good associate because you know they're already there; when they can take something and run with it; and when they're showing a lot of effort (and some results) in business development.

AN: We look primarily to whether an associate is able to first-chair a matter on their own and has the capability to generate meaningful business.

From a business perspective, what are you looking for in a partner?

SM: Because I do not have a business background, I would want someone with a business background or willing to hire someone with a business background to manage financials. I also would want someone who thinks of everyone in the office as a team, rather than people working "for" her. Also, firms should have a balance of "trees" people and "forest" people.

FR: Someone with meaningful relationships with potential referral sources.

DD: For us, it is a combo target number of working attorney receivables and business that you have brought in. In addition, your contributions to the firm and legal community at large are considered.

AN: Like most firms, my firm has a two-tier partnership. So senior associates need not have a book of business to make income partner, but rather need only demonstrate an ability and desire to generate business.

Do you actively set these expectations, or is it more of a passive approach as the associate develops?

SM: We are more passive, although we tend to eat lunch a lot, so we have an opportunity to evaluate.

FR: We make it clear to associates our expectations.

DD: The hard number goal to make shareholder is set by our board each year and is made known. Most of the encouragement/ expectations are communicated personally through discussions between associates and shareholders that they are close with. When I knew that my numbers were getting close, I actively sought out shareholders to discuss my desire to become a shareholder and get their feedback and advice.

AN: We actively set these expectations, but want associates to develop their skill set first and their business development skills second.

Should associates expect to be groomed for the transition?

SM: Yes. In our firm, I was given a one year "heads up" that the firm was considering me as shareholder. I began receiving financial reports at that point to help me see the financial aspects of the business.

DD: While our firm is clear that we would like for all of our associates to rise to partner someday, there is a lot of independent work that comes with that. I wasn't "groomed" in my opinion. I also did things on my own timeline – I became a shareholder ten years after joining the firm and twelve years after becoming a lawyer. During that time, I had two babies and didn't focus on business development until later than some of my colleagues. When I was ready, I sought out opportunities and spent a lot of time planning out how to meet my goal.

AN: To a certain extent, yes. We provide more responsibility as an associate becomes more senior, but it is incumbent upon associates to seek out a mentor and to inquire with partners about their progression.

What are indicators that an associate isn't preparing himself for partnership?

SM: I am unusual. I do NOT think working 8-5 means the associate is not preparing himself for partnership, depending on the work done. As mentioned above, the bigger indication is an associate not thinking beyond his or her cases.

FR: Someone who doesn't take ownership in their career.

DD: When they make no effort and show no interest in meeting new contacts and bringing in business. Also, when they don't seek out work or get to know partners outside of their group.

AN: It would raise red flags if an associate had low hours, had not developed a mentor relationship, had not developed key skill sets within her chosen practice area, or had poor client-relationship skills.

What practical things can an associate do on a daily or weekly basis to prepare himself for partnership?

SM: Read (case developments, business blogs, anything). Write (not just for cases, but articles or memos if you see a developing area of law or change in law that partners need to be aware of). Develop a relationship with co-workers, not just the partners, but include the partners.

FR: Get involved outside the firm and develop meaningful business relationships.

DD: Find out how your numbers work and how can you be more profitable to the firm. Find out expectations for those numbers and what other factors are included in the rubric. Tell partners that your goal is to make partner and get their advice and help. You will need advocates during the process.

AN: Stay in touch with law school friends and other potential business contacts (including junior in-house attorneys who you are working with). Develop and maintain these relationships so that you can capitalize on them as a senior associate or partner. In the meantime, focus on your craft. Get as much experience as possible, and be sure to develop working relationships with several partners in your firm's practice area. Be the "go to" associate that everyone wants to work with. That should help ensure a steady, and diverse, workflow.

While no two firms are the same, the responses of these lawyers iterate what I have long held and even shared on here about characteristics of developing associates. Namely, be mindful not only of your work but also of the firm's business and developing relationships with professionals in your practice area.

29

IMPROVING YOUR WRITING

CORRELATIONS BETWEEN WRITING AND RUNNING

B efore going to law school, I was a high school teacher. I stood in front of classrooms of kids all day. During the fall, I coached football. In the winter, I helped with the basketball program. In the spring, I went to many baseball games. And when on summer break, I framed houses or hanged gutter for friends of mine. I was active. I was in my 20s. It was easy to keep trim even though I didn't do any real exercise.

Then I went to law school in 2009, where I was sedentary. I sat for endless hours, listening or reading. And the weight started to creep up. By Christmas, it was noticeable. I was self-conscious about it and unhappy. I started going to the gym with my wife to work out. It helped some, but I *hated* working out at the gym. After several months, my wife mentioned she wanted to run a 5K. Neither of us had ever done any running before, but I decided I'd run with her. Anything to be out of that gym.

Little did I know I had traded one form of misery for another. We printed off a couch-to-5K regimen and began our training. Going from no cardio to running 3 times a week is hard. Even when those initial runs consist of little more than run for 1 minute, walk for 30 seconds; run for 2 minutes, walk for 1 minute; and so forth as you slowly, steadily build up your endurance. I did not enjoy learning to run ... at all. But I did prefer being outside to being in that dreaded gym.

By the time I could run 3 miles, I had decided that I liked running. In fact I decided I wanted to run a half marathon.

And 5 months later, I ran the Mercedes Half Marathon in Birmingham. Then I ran a few more races. The next year, my wife ran a half marathon with me at the Talladega Superspeedway. Running became an important part of my life over the next few years. And then we had a kid, and I haven't run regularly since. But I learned some important things along the way.

Muscle memory is an asset

When you first start running or even when you stretch yourself to run new distances, you don't know what to expect. You hold back somewhat on your tempo and exertion levels because you don't know what 3 miles or 6 miles or 13 miles feels like. But eventually you do it enough that when you set out to run a particular distance, your body knows what's coming. When I was conditioned well, I knew that running 3-4 miles at about an 8:00 minute mile would give me a pretty good workout. I could cruise through 6 miles at a 10:00/mi pace and feel good afterward. Even though I haven't run in about a year (which I'm more than a little ashamed to admit), I could go out right now and run 3 miles because my body still knows what that would take.

Writing requires the same training. If you had told me in 2016, when I launched my blog, that I would publish a 45,000 word book in 2018, I would have found that hard to believe. But I didn't have to write *Building a Better Law Practice* all at once. I had to write 800 words on one topic, 900 words on another topic. It took me a while to find my writing voice, but once I did, everything fell into place much more easily. I trained my brain how to think in a particular way so that now, when I sit down to write about a topic, I have muscle memory I can rely on.

Even on days when I'm not feeling particularly inspired or nothing seems to be falling into place well, I can push through the obstacles and get through the writing I need to do. This applies to legal writing, blogging, and creative writing. If you make a practice of writing regularly, you'll find your brain is a more finely tuned muscle that's able to respond upon demand.

Pacing yourself is the key

In 2012, I started running with my golden retriever. She loved it! Whenever she saw me getting my running shoes out of the closet, she would run around in circles, nipping at her tail, and barking at nothing. But for all her love of running, that dog was terrible at pacing herself. If we were going on a 4-miler, for the first half she was straining at the end of her leash, dragging me along with her. The second half of the run would find her lolling behind me, also at the end of her leash, but this time serving as an anchor rather than a propeller.

If you've got a big writing project ahead of you, whether it's an appellate brief or an article for a trade journal, you need to allot plenty of time to get it done. Unless you are well organized and in the regular practice of writing, you're not going to be able to write 7,000 words in a day.

Similarly, when I proposed *Building a Better Law Practice* to the ABA, I pitched it as a 28,000 word book. They replied they were interested in the book and liked the daily-reader format, but would only publish it if it were 40,000 words or more, and could I do that within the next four months? I replied of course I could do that! Never mind that it had taken me a year to come up with the first 28,000 words.

That conversation occurred in late November 2017. Knowing my January schedule was looking fairly rough, I figured out how often and how much I needed to write. Then in the early mornings on weekdays and during nap times on weekends, I wrote. I had plenty of ideas in my queue, where I drop ideas as they come to me. I knew that my schedule did not allot large chunks for writing time, so I had to be prepared and organized. And I had to pace myself.

Not only was there another 12,000 words (that become 17,000 words) to write, but there was also proofreading, editing, and re-writing to do ... multiple times. I had a long row to hoe, and if I didn't pace myself appropriately, I'd be lolling at the end of my leash, but with no one to pull me along.

The next time you set about on a large writing project, you'll find it much easier to accomplish if you're already in the regular habit of writing and plan appropriately to get your writing accomplished.

30

HOW TO ARGUE WITH OPPOSING COUNSEL

I n recent years, civil discourse has gone the way of the dodo bird. We seem societally incapable of contending with anyone who does not share our analysis or opinion. Rather than dealing with the merits of our opponent's argument, we are more likely to demean them and cast aspersions. Politics and social media serve up prime examples of these behaviors. But they don't end there. It has migrated into how we handle our cases.

By its nature, the law is a contentious business. But that doesn't mean we can't deal with each other in a civil manner, with integrity, and have productive discussions when we are at odds with one another. Our legal communities are small. If you approach every problem with a scorched-earth mentality, it won't be long until all that remains of your relationships with opposing counsel is charred bones and ash, and it is hard to have a productive relationship with a dead man.

I was recently handling a subrogation case arising out of a car wreck. Defense counsel was another insurance defense lawyer who I knew. Ultimately, it became clear to us his client was at fault for the accident. But there was a question of law about one of the items of damages we were claiming. The law surrounding the issue was pretty gray, allowing both of us to argue our positions with a straight face. We both laid out our positions through a series of emails, and ultimately, it became clear that either one of us could win or lose the argument depending on the judge's disposition.

As a disclaimer, not every legal position should be laid out so clearly for opposing counsel as we did here. But this time, we both knew we were likely settle, so hashing out our positions was the most effective way to resolve our differences and coming to a tenable agreement. Neither of us made our arguments personal or brought in outside issues to attempt to sway the outcome.

We treated each other with civility, which should be the norm in our interactions rather than the exception. We will all be better served by treating one another with respect, even when (or perhaps, especially when) we find ourselves at odds with one another.

How to argue effectively with opposing counsel

We will have plenty of opportunity to argue with opposing counsel about differences of opinion and interpretation. There is no shortage of that. But to do so effectively, it is important to remain focused on the issues and present meritorious, supported arguments. If you take bogus positions or make things personal, you will lose the respect of opposing counsel and sabotage a relationship.

It is important that we have functional relationships with the other side. We will be working with and against the same people for the entirety of our careers. We are best able to serve our clients' needs when we have a relationship with opposing counsel that enables us to navigate cases in a civil manner, trusting one another to play by the rules.

Even so, there will be times when you disagree and have irreconcilable interpretations of the facts or law. When these arguments arise, conduct yourself with propriety. Support your positions with evidence, statutes, and caselaw — and if your position doesn't have any support, perhaps you should reconsider it. And above all else, act with civility toward each other.

31

THE IMPORTANCE OF RETURNING PHONE CALLS

T his topic may seem elementary, but there's a reason professional athletes continue to work on the fundamentals of their game. It's important. Communication is fundamental to having a successful practice. Responding to emails and phone calls is an often underappreciated and overlooked area of professionalism and practice management. Here are three groups of people from whom you are likely receiving regular communications and to whom you should be responding promptly.

Responding to Judges

A judicial assistant called me and said, "I called you instead of the other lawyer because he never answers or calls me back."

I was befuddled. I knew that I had never been able to get him on the phone or received a return call from him, but I just could not believe the judge had the same experience.

I posted about this interaction on Twitter, with this recommendation, "You don't want to be the guy who never responds to the court's phone calls or emails." A sitting judge replied, "A big AMEN! I'm constantly surprised at the lack of response from lawyers to calls and emails." I had naively assumed that what the judicial assistant had told me was an anomaly. Apparently, there are some lawyers out there who feel no compulsion to respond to communication from the court.

Don't be that lawyer. Judges are people too. Sometimes the decisions they make are more or less coin tosses. If when they look down from their lofty perch what they see in you is someone who doesn't respect them enough to call them back or return emails to their staff, you can hazard a guess about how that ruling will land.

Responding to Lawyers

Sometimes in my cases, opposing counsel gets behind on responding to discovery. I'm not throwing stones here — we all get behind for one reason or another. Typically, when it's been a couple of weeks since the due date, I'll email opposing counsel saying something to the effect of, "Your discovery responses are overdue; let me know if you need an extension." I am generally fine with granting an extension of a couple of weeks when they respond, letting me know what they need. And in these situations, I will often even send a second letter if needed later.

There are other times though that opposing counsel does not respond to my overdue-discovery email. And they don't respond to the second email. Then they get fussy when I move to compel and have no trouble emailing or calling me about that.

Respond to the other lawyers in your life when they reach out to you. It is good for your relationships with each other. And it is good for your clients.

Responding to Clients

When I started practicing in 2012, one of the first and most important things my mentor taught me was this: if a client calls, answer the phone. I know — really groundbreaking stuff. But there will be times you are either away from the phone or just unable to answer. The corollary lesson was this: if a client sends you an email or leaves a voicemail, you should respond within 24 hours, even if it is just to say, "I'm looking into this and will get back to you." This has become standard operating procedure for me over the last six years.

Your clients are the lifeblood of your practice. Without clients, you don't get to practice law. If your clients are calling you, it's likely because they need something. The thing they need may seem insignificant to me or you. They may just want to know about the status of their case. Or they may have important information to relay that changes the trajectory of the case. But the point is you won't know unless you return your client's correspondence.

If they often do not hear back from you, they will find another lawyer to do their work. Your clients have never had more options for hungry lawyers than they do now. And it's never been easier for your clients to find a new lawyer. Clients who believe their correspondence or phone calls are going into an abyss are unhappy clients. And unhappy clients don't stick around.

I have two clients that have begun sending me much more work over the last two years, largely because of my regular and meaningful communication with them. They have other firms they use in the state. They have more experienced lawyers on their panel counsel list. But they also know that when they send work to me, they will have access to me when they need it.

Your clients have choices about who to send their work to. Give them reasons to send it to you.

32

REPLY ALL SHOULD NOT BE YOUR DEFAULT EMAIL RESPONSE

I was involved in a multiparty email exchange about a pretrial scheduling order. As sometimes happens in conversations among many lawyers about how much time to allot to discovery, expert disclosures, and dispositive motion deadlines, things went a little sideways. And since all this communication was by email, no one could read anyone's tone, and each inferred the worst from the other parties.

Everyone was sitting in his or her own office getting progressively more frustrated. I got an email from one lawyer putting opposing counsel on blast. Just really letting him have it. The allegations were that he was bad at his job and his client would be best served by firing him. He was lazy and incompetent. And he was a total moron.

Then I noticed the contents of the To and CC boxes. The sender had hit REPLY ALL. Everyone in the email chain had the joy of reading his email and knowing he had unwittingly exposed his innermost loathing to everyone. You'll not be surprised to learn that we didn't succeed in agreeing to the proposed scheduling order.

REPLY ALL is an option, but shouldn't be the default

You and I both know people who use REPLY ALL as their default email response. Usually, it's in response to a listserv email for whom the original sender is the only person interested in the response. But it's a terrible habit that can result in ... unfortunate and unforeseen consequences. Don't be *that guy* who uses REPLY ALL as your default email response. REPLY ALL should be the exception, not the rule, when it comes to responding to emails.

Here's a good rule of thumb: never put anything in an email that you wouldn't want read back to you by a judge or in a deposition. That's a good rule to live by. Keep it in mind next time you want to send a nasty email. You likely don't want that made an exhibit to a motion.

33

KEEPING UP WITH TIME ENTRIES AND TO-DO LISTS

I n our line of work, time is money, so I keep close track of my billable hours. I write my time entries down after each billable event. When I hear about lawyers not writing down time for a couple of days and having to go back and recreate it, I shudder. People are generally lousy judges of how long it takes to accomplish tasks.

When lawyers go back and recreate time, they are sure to overbill clients for some tasks while underbilling other clients for different tasks. Not to mention the things they've done and forgotten about in the last 24-48 hours. No matter how it turns out, someone is getting cheated out of time or money.

Have a system for documenting time entries

Since my first day of practice, I have used the same method of recording my time entries. I keep a yellow 5x8 steno pad to the right of my mouse and write down every billable task as I do it. During the week, my notepad goes with me nearly everywhere I go. At least anywhere I'll be long enough to check email, answer a phone call, or write notes down.

Later, I enter those time entries into an Excel spreadsheet. My assistant then takes those spreadsheets and drops those time entries into our billing software.

While redundant, my system has the benefit of having one hard copy of my billable time in case something tragic happens to our computer systems (I have every notepad that I've filled out beginning in 2012. They're moldering in some desk drawer and I feel oddly sentimental about them.), as well as two digital copies of those same time entries — one in Excel and another in the billing software.

There are many effective methods of keeping track of time, and I'm not advocating that mine is the best. New programs will sync Siri or Alexa to billing software and allow you to dictate your time entries directly into the software. One of my partners keeps his billing software open all day on a second monitor and types up his time entries as he goes along. My point is that whatever method you use to record your billable time, you need to have a system you abide by that doesn't allow you to lose unrecorded time or force you to recreate it sometime later.

Managing your to-do lists

My practice involves a large volume of personal auto and general liability cases. Most of these cases involve many of the same tasks in each case with little variation. Because of the volume, of all the things I discuss in this book that are most capable of getting my practice out of control and resulting in me being reactionary and putting out fires rather than proactively managing my caseload, it is letting my to-do list get out of sorts.

I use a color-coded system to identify what tasks have yet to be done, are pending, or still need to be done. For example, if I haven't issued discovery requests yet, I'll have a red marker over that cell. Once the discovery requests have been filed but before I have received the responses, the cell will be yellow or orange (once the responses are overdue). When the written discovery is completed, those cells will be green.

But there are plenty of tasks that fall outside the scope of my case management spreadsheet. For these things, I have a to-do list. I love to-do lists, mostly because I really enjoy crossing things off to-do lists. In fact, I've been known to put an item on a to-do list so that moments later when I complete the task, I can have the joy of crossing it off the list.

I write my to-do lists on a white 5x8 steno notepad that is the sibling of the yellow notepad for time entries. Again, this is the same method I've used since I started practicing. As with recording billable hours, there are many methods for making to-do lists. You can use Evernote, an app on your phone, or practice management software. As technology progresses, your options for systematically managing your to-do list will also increase. However you choose to keep up with the tasks you need to accomplish to keep your practice in order, make sure to be organized and consistent.

The more consistently you implement the systems you have in place to manage your practice, the more efficient you will be and the less likely you are to allow important events to fall through the cracks. Your case management systems can be complicated, but need not be — they can be as simple as having two different color notebooks that you keep attached to your hip.

34

TRACKING THE VALUE OF YOUR BILLABLE HOURS

O ne of the major determinants for how an associate's year-end review will go is how much money she made for the firm. There are other things too, like how an associate is developing client and case management skills and whether the associate is developing her own book of business. But when everything is boiled down to its rawest form, partners at most firms want to know how profitable the associate is.

Since an associate's profitability is the most important thing to her employer, she should make it a priority to know this information herself. But I recommend that she not only know the information for a year-end meeting, but monitor it throughout the year.

Keeping track of your billable hours

Most of us have a pretty good idea of what our billable requirements are. But do you know how much that translates to in actual dollars? Do you know your hourly rates? Do you know what your share of the overhead is so that you can determine how profitable you are? Does your firm allow you access to this information?

Since I started practicing in 2012, I have always kept thorough track of my billable time entries on a daily, monthly, and annual basis. I'm a sucker for spreadsheets, so I created a spreadsheet that would help me keep up with my time on an ongoing basis.

Only recently did I realize I was missing an important column. A column for the *value* of my billable hours. I was not keeping track of how much money those billable hours translated to. This is important because time entries don't always tell the whole picture.

Monitoring the value of your billable hours

Some firms allow you to write down time for attending CLEs or marketing events. If you go to an all-day CLE, you may get to write down 7.0 hours for this day. Or if you travel to Chicago to pitch a new client or build your relationship with an existing client, you write down 18.0 hours for your travel/meeting time. Your monthly hours total will still look great, but while those are essential to your business, the hours you spend doing those things did not earn the firm any revenue. If you are only keeping up with your time entries (like I was), you will miss a vital piece of information. You don't know how much money your cumulative time is worth.

In a meeting with one of the partners at my firm, we were talking about larger goals for the futures of the firm and me, and how billables affected those things. He recommended that rather than shooting for an hourly goal each day, I have a goal to bill a particular amount of money each day. Doing so would put me in a better position to reach my goals.

Because I already had a spreadsheet for my time entries, all I had to do was add a column to my spreadsheet and plug in an easy formula that would allow me every day as I entered my time to see how much money my time entries amounted to. [Note: Time entries and billable rate are to illustrate only and do not reflect actual events.]

Client File No.	Case Name	Description	Time	Value
001-001	Dewey v. Decimal	Prepare for taking plaintiff's deposition	1.2	$ 240.00
001-002	Kennedy v. Oswalt	Draft responses to interrogatories	0.7	$ 140.00
001-002	Kennedy v. Oswalt	Draft Motion for HIPAA Protective Order and proposed order	0.4	$ 80.00
001-001	Dewey v. Decimal	Attend and conduct Plaintiff's deposition	2.3	$ 460.00
001-002	Kennedy v. Oswalt	Review, analysis, and notes re Plaintiff's medical records	0.8	$ 160.00
001-003	Jackson v. Boswell	Phone conference with client re discovery	0.3	$ 60.00

As you can see, this is a pretty straightforward spreadsheet. There are only five columns. The first two identify the file number and name. The third reflects the work I performed. Column D enumerates the increments of time each task took. Column E is the new column — it shows the monetary value of each task.

If you are not proficient with Microsoft Excel, here is what the formula looks like to derive that value: =sum([insert cell value here]*[insert hourly rate here]). Here's the sample: =sum(d4*200).

The importance of knowing your revenue generation

Your value to your firm is directly tied to how much revenue you generate. I assure you that your firm knows how much money you are making for them. If you want to be on equal footing at your year-end meeting or if you want to advocate for a raise, you need documentation to support your position. You may be like me and be at a firm that treats you well and have people around you who are interested in your well-being, but that comfort level is not a good reason to be unknowledgeable about the business side of things.

If your firm has goals for you or you have goals for yourself, the best way to make sure you are moving toward accomplishing those goals is to regularly monitor your progress. Keeping track of the monetary value of your billable hours is one of the most effective ways to monitor your profitability and position yourself for success within your firm.

35

HOW TO FEEL COMFORTABLE IN YOUR PRACTICE

BUT AVOID THE DUNNING-KRUGER EFFECT

I t occurred to me a few months ago, while working on a problem no one in my firm had dealt with before, that I had just entered my seventh year of practice. That suddenly seemed like a pretty significant amount of time, which started me on a pig trail thinking about how comfortable I am daily with my knowledge and experience levels. Because I was also curious about how comfortable others with similar experience levels were with their practices, I ran a poll on Twitter and LawyerSmack, asking this question, "For those who have been practicing 6-9 years, how do you feel on a daily basis?"

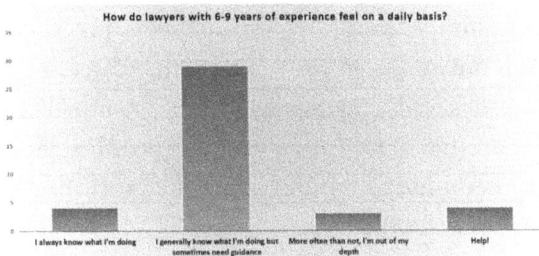

How do lawyers with 6-9 years of experience feel on a daily basis?

Feeling Comfortable in Your Practice

The result was about what I expected. Most of us feel like by and large, we have a pretty good handle on things but sometimes need a helping hand.

Most of my work is pretty well contained within a couple of tort-related practice areas. For the last couple of years, the bulk of my practice has been defending personal and commercial auto cases. Within that line of work, I am usually comfortable and have a good grasp of the caselaw, how to evaluate cases, and how to work up and (if the client wants) try a case. But once every month or two, I'll run across some obscure issue that forces me either to do some legal research or reach out to others in my office to see if they've dealt with this same issue before.

I work for other clients who write broader lines of insurance for businesses. When they come calling, I never know whether I'm going to be dealing with allegations of negligent failure to repair a tractor, a slip-and-fall, or a fire loss caused by a faulty heater. When I get one of these calls, the first thing I do is get excited - I love the variety. The next thing is to do a quick assessment of whether this is something I can handle on my own or need to bring in one of my partners with more experience dealing with these particular issues.

That said, the prideful part of me still bucks against asking for help. It tells me I can handle it on my own. But the client-oriented part jumps in and suggests that while I could probably figure things out and even get a fair result, I can't likely do it as effectively or efficiently managing the case by myself. I've found that clients are far more receptive to lawyers bringing in help rather than floundering around while they sort through issues and gain a proper footing.

Avoiding the Dunning-Kruger Effect

One of the most important parts of becoming an experienced practitioner is knowing what you don't know and having the meekness to bring in more resources. One lawyer responded to my Twitter poll: "I know what I don't know in my cases and have enough experience to see how it will end badly, and only more work will hedge against terrible outcomes."

If you don't have the self-awareness to see your own weaknesses, you're likely suffering from the Dunning-Kruger Effect, in which underperformers assess themselves as being much better at their work than they are. In their paper "Unskilled and Unaware of It," Professors Dunning and Kruger expressed the following idea: "[T]he knowledge and intelligence that are required to be good at a task are often the same qualities needed to recognize that one is not good at that task—and if one lacks such knowledge and intelligence, one remains ignorant that one is not good at that task."

There are ways to make sure you are not falling victim to a sense of false confidence. Perform objective self-analysis by having something to compare yourself against. Be receptive to feedback and constructive criticism, and implement proposed changes to improve your work. Make regular, purposeful efforts to educate yourself on your practice areas and stay abreast of new developments.

You can be assured of one thing though: in the practice of law, when you start to get too confident, some jury or bizarre issue or difficult client will come along to swipe your feet out from under you to bring you back down to earth a bit.

36

LEAVE THE JOB YOU HATE AND LAND THE JOB YOU WANT (PART 1)

I f you are a lawyer who's been grinding away for a couple of years at a job that makes you miserable, a job you hate, then you need to read this. Stop whatever else you are doing and receive some hope and encouragement.

Maybe you don't know there are other options. Perhaps you don't think you are good enough. Possibly, the money is too good to pass up where you are now. I will tell you this, and it is the same thing I've been telling people since I started teaching high school in 2004: no amount of money is worth you being miserable at the thought of going to work every day.

If you are one of those lawyers unhappy with your situation, you don't need the most vibrant personality or longest resume to start looking around for a different job. What you need is the fortitude to pursue what you want, the wherewithal to grab hold of an opportunity that presents itself to you, and (not to be underestimated) the ability to act appropriately and not present yourself like a total weirdo. Leave the job you hate to find more fulfilling work.

These are the experiences of lawyers who were unhappy in

the job situation and took the initiative to find work that was more satisfying to them.

Grab hold of the opportunities you make

Martha: I quit my life in Houston but couldn't find anything else because I was only two years out and my experience was all criminal prosecution. My dad lives in D.C. He was like, "It's a whole city of lawyers - there has to be SOMETHING?" So I moved up here and spent a year in his basement. Got lots of rejections which was neat.

One day I was bitching on Twitter and someone DM'ed me to ask what I wanted to do. I said defense policy. In undergrad I focused on war/strategy/conflict, etc. With a military dad and veteran/legislator grandpa, I was born for PoliSci nerdery. I went to law school thinking I'd learn the legal half of those issues, and LOL @ ME, I started in 2009, when there were no jobs.

So being in D.C. was my chance to do what I'd *wanted* to do from the beginning. She happened to know a guy who did defense policy work. She put us in touch. I got lunch with him, and I was basically like, "How do I do what *you* do?" Turns out his boss needed an intern. I started three years ago and now I'm our director of operations, and also have a few clients I handle.

Part of my work now is drafting whitepapers and memos, making PowerPoint presentations for my boss (the primary lobbyist) to take to the Hill, writing letters for or to congress-folk. I could have done this job having gotten a master's in government stuff, but to be honest I'm glad I got a JD and glad I practiced for a bit.

Never burn your bridges

JD: I was a litigation associate for six years. Loved the firm and trial work. Hated the BS that comes with litigation and a lot of cases that came my way for being low on the totem pole. I was stressed out and carrying work with me everywhere. You know how it is grinding in a firm as a litigation associate.

I switched to in-house at the end of last year and it has been night-and-day in terms of stress and life balance/happiness. I am doing more transactional work and also managing outside counsel on litigation. I papered the city to death for about 1-2 years, getting offers and also interviews. I turned the offers down because I didn't like the fit. I landed my current job through networking via the manager at my old job before law school.

I saw the posting and realized the manager had a connection with our chief legal officer. It got my foot in the door and I got the offer. My resume didn't even make the cut initially and didn't even land on her desk. If not for the connection, I would not have received an interview.

The message that I would share with readers is: Don't get discouraged if you don't land another offer right away. Keep applying and looking for new opportunities. Relationships are important too, so never burn bridges.

Weigh the risks and rewards

Matt: I left the firm I was at for five years, joined two friends from school at their firm, and added my name on the door. I couldn't be happier now. I do not advise people to do this without some planning. It is not as easy as I may make it sound. I'll just say that I was in a fortunate position to be able to do that. I don't have anyone depending on my income (kids) and I left my old firm with over 100 open cases and about 150 clients. I was in a fortunate position. If I had kids, I may not have done it. If I didn't have all those open cases, I would have been super broke for a few months, maybe more.

Do your homework and persevere through setbacks

Elizabeth: I was working at a firm library — big for its market, but it was one large office in the state's largest city and a tiny office in the state capital. It was really busy; it had just grown its IP practice (from one to seven attorneys, with more practice areas) and had instituted a new procedure for conflict checks that involved the library.

I had temp'ed there for a while and I liked the firm culture. It seemed stable and cohesive, and while there were definitely some attorneys people tiptoed around, all in all, people worked hard and were good to each other. However, that changed. It was subtle, with no one thing I could point to as an illustration, but in general it became pretty tense and seemed less cohesive, and I felt uncomfortable.

Plus, I wanted to teach and the local environment was trying to kill me (allergies). So I decided that I needed to get out. The problem was that there were a lot fewer academic jobs there than were in the Bay Area. Step 1 became: 'Get back to the Bay Area.'

I interviewed for a contracting job where I was hired 24 hours after the phone interview. I had a month to move between states, and a week of that would be spent out of town/the country. I did that, with a lot of help from my spouse. A month after my interview, I was at a new job in a different state.

After four months, I assessed whether I wanted to stay

where I was and for how long. This firm didn't have the tension of my old one, but it felt much less cohesive. And I still wanted to teach. So I started looking around in terms of academia. The Bay Area has seven law schools. That was a benefit. But a drawback was that there is a particular set of skills that people tend to have when working in different parts of academic libraries. It's very segmented and very deep, and I did not have *that* experience, despite working in an academic library before law school.

Luck came my way again - my law school alma mater was hiring, and the contact remembered me. I asked if I would be seriously considered if I applied, and she said yes. So I started preparing – DM'ing experts on Twitter, reading blogs, putting together outlines and resource binders. I got to the all-day interview, powered through the flop sweat and dry mouth and four different interviews plus a presentation and lunch with these people. And I didn't get the job.

I couldn't really blame them, as I didn't have that exact experience that niche academic libraries typically look for. But now I had all of this research. And somehow I parlayed it into doing an out-of-state CLE, and I started thinking about doing a podcast and building up my authority cred.

And then, I get a call offering me the job - the other candidate turned it down. So luck again. And now I am here. In academia, about to teach my first course, and I like it so much. But to encapsulate - it took a fair bit of risk, a lot of family support, more than a little luck, and a readiness to pounce and prepare when risk and luck paid off.

Some people have a bad experience and conclude they don't like being a lawyer. But that might not be the case at all. It may be instead they didn't like that particular role or employer. By putting themselves in a new environment, they may discover joy or satisfaction they were previously unaware is available to them.

37

LEAVE THE JOB YOU HATE AND LAND THE JOB YOU WANT (PART 2)

A s more evidence that the fit at your job is as important as the work you're doing, I wanted to share with you Kate's and Bob's stories as well. They bolster this idea that you can leverage your relationships into the job that best fits your personality and temperament.

Relationships are key to business success

Kate: When I was miserable, I started reaching out to colleagues and older lawyers and kind of politely venting to see if what I was experiencing was just the pains of being a lawyer or if my problems were uniquely related to my firm. I wasn't positive I wanted to leave my firm necessarily. I was actually thinking I needed to quit law because it wasn't for me.

After a few lunches, I knew I was miserable because of my firm, so I reached out to a few connections - partners at firms who I knew from mentoring or summer clerkships. Reaching out to people for advice kind of converted into job hunting when I realized I didn't need to quit law.

The partner I had clerked under at a large local firm had left and opened a new branch of a larger regional firm. I approached him mainly for the connections, hoping for an email introduction to other firms in town that might be hiring. He ended up recruiting me to work for him.

Keep your connections fresh. Even though I was no-offered at a large local firm, I still ended up being able to use that clerkship for something.

Finding the right fit may take some effort

Bob: I'm an attorney with four years of experience who moved diagonally through several jobs to finally make it to one that fits me and uses my strengths. It can be done. My last job (and the last few before that), I liked the work, but management was unresponsive at best and abusive at worst. Hundred-hour weeks, verbal abuse, unclear or inconsistent job expectations, lack of management support, a total lack of recourse, the whole schmear. It took enough of a toll on my physical and mental health that I knew I had to get a better job.

If all you want is *a* job, you can get *a* job. You probably have *a* job. The trick is getting one that suits you. Know what you want, know your strengths, and let other people know. The first two are necessary prerequisites.

I wanted a job with semi-predictable hours, a reasonable salary, and responsive management, that I could reasonably argue was serving a public good. I could litigate but strongly preferred not to. I'm flexible in terms of practice area—I'm not attached to a particular area, and I learn systems quickly, often quickly enough to teach others. I'm easy to work with and pretty personable; one of the benefits of having a lot of disparate work experience and hobbies is that you can talk to anyone about anything.

Once you know your strengths, take a look at your resume. It should tell a story that shows your achievements and trends over your career. This is important because you're a lawyer—everyone has a doctorate, and all your first year's experience are grunt work. Sorry. But by now, you know your strengths (see above!), so play them up, and give your resume that third dimension that helps you stand out. My resume shows that I've switched practice areas twice since being licensed, learned quickly enough to get promoted to management positions, and improved performance metrics in several areas while delivering quality work.

After that, letting people know your wants and strengths is relatively straightforward. Choose who you let know. I got my current job by taking a broad but targeted and efficient approach to applications. Based on my wants and my strengths, I knew in-house was likely a good fit. I focused my applications on in-house and JD-advantage jobs, figuring that a good work environment would be an acceptable trade-off if I had to change fields again.

I wallpapered the Internet with my resume and stalked LinkedIn to find connections who might be able to get my story in front of the right people. I also had relatives and friends I'd made through college, law school, Twitter, LawyerSmack, who were shopping my resume around. Since I'd given them targets and an easy narrative hook to sell me, it wasn't a huge ask. I eventually got in a room with a few hiring managers, got an offer, and it's been a great experience since.

Choosing who to let know is where things can really get interesting. I got an interview with a recruiting firm by drawing a guy on Twitter as a cartoon bird carrying a bazooka. (No kidding.) But that's an example of someone finding out about my strengths (easy to work with, personable, committed to quality work) who got hooked into finding out more. Once I told him I was a lawyer looking for work, flexible, and quick to learn, he sent my resume to my area's branch of his recruiting firm. It didn't pan out, but not everything needs to. All you need is one.

And for the love of Mike, have savings. Folk wisdom has it that you should have six months worth of expenses saved for emergencies. A job sucking the life from you is an emergency. It takes time to find one that's a good fit, and not having savings means you don't have the leverage to reject a bad fit.

There are so many avenues for getting out of the job you hate and into the job you want. Everyone featured here used different methods of obtaining the satisfying work they're in now. I want you to understand there are both traditional and out-of-the-box ways to find work and getting out of the job that's making you miserable. It will take effort, perseverance, and using the connections you've made, but what you're looking for is out there. And if it's not, blaze a new path and create it.

38

SHOULD LAWYERS TALK TO RECRUITERS ABOUT JOB OPPORTUNITIES?

Some time ago, I got a message on LinkedIn from a headhunter asking if she could talk to me about an available job with another firm in town. I was happy where I was and not interested in moving, but I told her I would talk to her anyway. I have long operated by a philosophy that I will not blindly turn away an opportunity.

The next day she called and told me all about the job opportunity. She then asked what it would take to get me away from my current firm. I told her what a difficult question that is because of all the things I like about my current situation:

"I bill a lot of hours, but I'm able to work with a lot of autonomy. My firm gives me the support I need to develop my own business. No one is taking roll every day to make sure we're at our desks from 8:00-5:00; if I need to leave at 3:00 for childcare reasons, no one is going to harass me about that. I'm surrounded by good people who are good lawyers."

When I finished telling her about my firm, the recruiter sat silently on the other end of the phone for a minute before saying, "So you're telling me it would take a unicorn." The rest of our conversation was pretty short after that. The job she was calling about was just a regular workhorse. No horns or magical powers.

Why Should Lawyers Talk to Recruiters?

There are two reasons lawyers should talk to recruiters if called: networking and understanding your market value.

You should always be open to expanding your professional network. The legal job market can be volatile, and you never know when someone you've met along the way may be able to help you at a later time. It's possible my situation at my current firm could change — a major client could leave resulting in insufficient work, or leadership could shift causing an unpleasant environment — and I could need a way out. If I haven't taken the opportunity to meet people and hear their offers even when I was content with my situation, then I'm not going to have any resources available when I'm looking to make a change.

Understanding your market value can be tricky, especially as you become an older associate and near the practice length where you expect to receive a partnership offer. Hopefully, you are at a place where there's a clear path to partnership and open dialogue about what is necessary for you to make partner. But even if you are, no two firms are alike. Your value at one firm may not reflect what it would be at another. The best way to understand your worth is to have conversations with recruiters and headhunters who fit lawyers to job opportunities. They, more than anyone else, can aid you in self-evaluation of your skills to pair it with your appropriate place in the market.

How Should Firms Feel about Their Lawyers Talking to Recruiters?

While I am advocating here that you should hear out folks who approach you with opportunities, that advice comes with the disclaimer that not all firms will appreciate your doing so. There are certainly firms that will put a lawyer on the curb who is audacious enough to hear out another job offer, so you should be mindful of that, if you are at a firm likely to have those sentiments.

I firmly believe that law firms should not be averse to their lawyers talking to recruiters. First, a firm should be developing good lawyers, so that other firms recognize your firm as a breeding ground for talent. You want to be the kind of firm from which other firms are trying to hire your lawyers. There's a maxim that's been floating around the internet for years with no clear source of attribution; a CFO comments to the CEO, "What happens if we train our employees and they leave?" The CEO replies, "What happens if we don't and they stay?" Law firms receive no higher compliment about the people who work for them than knowing that others want to poach their lawyers.

Second, if firms are developing good lawyers who they want to retain, they should have the environment and compensation structure to keep those lawyers around. There will always be some attrition. Some people are always looking for the next, best thing that they think is just beyond the horizon. But there are as many people who are reluctant to leave a good situation. So a firm with a good atmosphere that pays its people fairly should be confident enough to allow its people to talk to recruiters and accept the compliment that they raised up another good attorney who is coveted by other firms.

39

FIND A COMMUNITY TO HELP YOU GROW

T here is an adage that applies to lawyers as much as it does to families: "It takes a village to raise a child." Sure you can try to go from being a baby lawyer to an adolescent lawyer to fully matured on your own. You can try doing it without a mentor to help you and without a community to support you. But why would you want to?

Traditional Sources of Community for Lawyers

It used to be that you were limited by geography to finding and participating in a community. Local bar associations played a huge role in the lives of many lawyers, acting as sources of referrals and collegiality. Many have continued to serve this important function, but lawyers are no longer limited to traditional communities like this.

More recently, practice-oriented organizations have provided additional avenues for growth, development, and community. Conferences provide opportunities for lawyers to discuss common problems, learn methods of improving their practice, and meet new people. But aside from exchanging messages on a listserv or attending meetings a couple of times a year, these interactions are often fairly limited. Most of us need something more consistent and readily available.

Maybe you have that among a group of friends who you can bounce ideas off of. But from what I've seen, most lawyers do not. Their daily or weekly interactions are constrained to the folks within their own firms. Or if they're lucky, perhaps they have a mentor available to them.

Find Your Community of Lawyers

Technology has created new opportunities for networking and developing communities. Two years ago, I found a community in LawyerSmack that has been both helpful and a source of great entertainment. We have a group of people rooting for each other to succeed, are willing to share practice ideas, empathize with each other through family problems, and refer business to each other. It is a place where colleagues can become friends despite being separated by hundreds of miles. Here is an example of where the community helped out one of the members who had career advice questions:

Matt: Hey guys, interview etiquette question and I'm curious what the LawyerSmack thoughts are. I'm interviewing for a public interest place that seems like it lines up perfectly with my interests and experience. The salary range they posted is below what I'm making now and well below what I want to make. I applied anyway and had a great phone interview and they want me to come in to meet with the director. I know I can't accept the job at the range they listed. Originally, I figured I'd go and if they really wanted me, we can negotiate but my girlfriend thinks that it may come across really bad that I wasted their time with the entire process if I could never accept anything within the range they posted. Thoughts? Should I just cancel the interview?

For clarification, the range they posted was small (5k difference between high and low) and I'm being paid about 10k more than the top of their range right now.

Nick: Unless there are some major long-term bridges being burned, you owe them no duty to cancel the meeting. It's their responsibility prior to bringing you in to determine if you're willing to work for that salary — you're not wasting their time; they're wasting their own time.

Walter: As someone who ran a nonprofit for a bit (and has interviewed for a number of both non-legal and legal positions), a lot of times more $$ can be found if they really want you. That being said, I would expect that you are going to make a bit less than you are now. I don't think you need to cancel the interview — if nothing else you can always say, "The fit isn't right given the salary," or something similar.

Matt: Got it. Yeah all of that makes sense. Thanks, guys. I wasn't planning to cancel but wanted to check just in case if I was out of line.

Erica: Yeah I'd ask for more but be prepared for, "No."

Keith: Yeah, no reason not to go. But you've also got to look out for yourself and your family. The work might be more satisfying, but if you can't support yourself, that's a no go.

Dan: It might be reasonable to think about telling them you can't accept the job for less than $X - do they still want you to interview?

Matt: I was thinking about that. But I think it might come across as a little pretentious?

Jeremy: I agree with what has been posted. Go to the interview and allow them to tell you no.

Dan: The real question is why you applied to a job with a posted salary range well below what you would expect.

Kristen: Yeah. I think you go, and if you get an offer, take a day or two to think, call back and say — this is a perfect fit for me, I'd love to do it, I don't think I can justify the financial cut, blah blah blah.
    He just said why. He wants the job and hopes there's wiggle room.

Dan: Eh, I expect the place will offer him a job, he'll tell them their salary demands, and they'll go, well, why'd you bother? We told you what we were paying.

Kristen: Maybe.

Jeremy: A posted salary range is always negotiable if they want you. I would not not respond to a posting because of salary.

Walter: Agreed, Jeremy.

Kristen: But maybe they call him back in 9 months after it doesn't work out with a new guy, too.

Matt: Yeah, I applied because it matched up perfectly with my experience, and I figured they'd be willing to negotiate a bit above what they posted for a perfect match. I'm not asking for double the salary or anything.

Kristen: I don't think you need to justify that. It makes sense.

Craig: Oh, come on, Dan, you know it's more flexible than that.

Matt: It's about teaching kids law and running mock trial programs and stuff, and I've been coaching mock trial and moot court since college, and I'm involved in multiple programs today as a volunteer. So I can't imagine another candidate with that kind of experience also applying. I figure they might be willing to be flexible.

Dan: My suggestion was to simply inform them ahead of time of your salary expectations. Because they'll offer you the job and then get whiplash

Kristen: I've been on interviews before with a posted range and then they've been like, "So what are your salary expectations?" [shrugs shoulders]

Anyway. Go and kill it. And if it doesn't work out, no big deal.

Matt: Thanks everyone! This has been really helpful.

What a Community Can Do for You

The point here isn't how great LawyerSmack is ... although it is. But you need a group of people around you who can help you when you have questions. Who can disagree with you and question your ideas. Who can support you. Who you can talk about whether hotdogs are sandwiches with.

We all need support, encouragement, and entertainment. Find a community of lawyers that can help you grow. Whether it's lawyers in your practice area who are spread across the country or a diverse group of lawyers you eat lunch with weekly. And if you can't *find* a group that meets your particular needs, form one.

40

BEING SMART ISN'T AS IMPRESSIVE AS YOU THINK

Certain things matter more to me than I care to admit.[1] Chief among them have been my accomplishments when compared to my peer group and how I am perceived by others. Along these lines, I used to place a lot of value in being described as smart.

When I was a baby lawyer being introduced to a client by one of the partners, he described me as one of our our smartest associates. I thought my heart would explode with pride. After my initial internal dialogue of "Wow! That's awesome," my next thought was, "I'm not sure that's true." But even if it were true, is that how I want to be known?

Not that it's bad to be known as smart, but over the course of time, I've decided that *smart* is not the first trait I want people to associate me with. There is nothing I have done of my own accord to have whatever amount of intelligence that has been bestowed upon me. Being smart is kind of like being good looking (which I'm not laying any claim to). It is certainly helpful and you'd probably rather have it than not, but there is nothing you've done to deserve it.

"I don't care about seeming smart. I think that's overvalued."
Stephen Dubner, co-author of *Freakonomics*

Now don't get me wrong, being a lawyer requires a certain minimum threshold of intelligence. Some practice areas even require more intelligence than others. By and large the institutional barriers to entry usually do a fair job of weeding out those who lack the intellectual incapacity to perform the critical thinking necessary for lawyers. So I'm not saying being smart isn't important. It's just that it doesn't really say all that much about you.

Another reason I've mentally de-emphasized the importance I place on being recognized as smart is there is always someone else smarter. In high school and college, I had to study some, but I don't recall things being all that difficult most of the time — except for calculus and trigonometry, but that's why I'm a lawyer and not in STEM. I expect most of you can identify with that. When I got into grad school, I really had to put in some hours reading and writing, but still found myself among equals.

Then I went to law school, where I found that I was what I think of as normal-people smart. There I encountered some folks who are freakishly smart. The kind of people who you can mostly understand what they're pontificating about, but it takes burning some calories to rev your brain up that high. Years later, I've joined LawyerSmack and follow #lawtwitter, where I daily bear witness to discussions among lawyers whose intelligence far surpasses my own.

But I am not discouraged by this anymore. Instead, I am latching onto the coattails of those who can help me increase both the breadth and depth of my knowledge. Similarly, I have peers who have accomplished more than I have. And I strive not to envy them. Their accomplishments do not diminish my own. There is room for all of us to have success.

So I don't want to be known as the smartest lawyer at my firm. It is a label that has no intrinsic value. It is like the athlete who is described as having "so much potential," which means nothing if he does not capitalize on it.

I would be much better served being known as the most trustworthy or most client-oriented lawyer, or perhaps even wisest or most ambitious. These are descriptors that reveal character, which can be supported (or not) by a person's actions. They reflect a person who is known by things he has done, rather than just revealing the observation of an inborn trait.

I have taken a long time to recognize, then reprioritize these values. Maybe this can help you get a jump on identifying the characteristics for which you want to be recognized, then begin taking actions that will enable others to see those qualities in you.

41

APOLOGIZE WHEN YOU ACT LIKE A JERK

I n January 2018, in the middle of the college football national championship game, Nick Saban substituted out his quarterback Jalen Hurts, who had led Alabama to its second consecutive national title game. Saban sent in his true freshman quarterback Tua Tagovailoa, who by all accounts was expected to be the next great quarterback. In the final moments of the game with Alabama trailing, Tua delivered a strike to his wide receiver for the game-winning touchdown.

For the next eight months, something of a quarterback controversy brewed in Tuscaloosa. For the 2018 season, would Alabama's quarterback be the junior who had led the team for two years or the young QB who had won the hearts and imaginations of fans over the course of two quarters of football? And it was this question that hounded Nick Saban in every interview he gave over that time.

Ultimately, Tagovailoa started the season opener in 2018 and again led Alabama to a victory, this time over Louisville. After the game, sideline report Maria Taylor asked Saban what he had learned about his quarterback situation. He responded poorly: "Well, I still like both guys. I think both guys are good players. I think both guys can help our team, alright? So why do you continually try to get me to say something that doesn't respect one of them? I'm not going to. So quit askin'!"

A short time later, Saban called Taylor and apologized for his bad behavior. Then he addressed it at his press conference and took ownership for his inappropriate response.

This is an example of exactly what should happen when you behave badly. You show contrition and offer an apology to the person toward whom your words or actions were directed. What you should not do is make excuses for your bad acts.

Do not excuse your bad behavior

I was at a docket call recently with a judge whose assistant is notorious for sending nasty emails and cussing lawyers who don't do things the way she likes. Before the judge entered the courtroom, she made us all be quiet and listen to her describe, then excuse, her own bad behavior.

She told the room full of lawyers the reason she acted as she does is that she wants to "mentor" lawyers. Not every lawyer has someone to show them the way, so she has placed that mantle upon herself. She said she knows people forward her emails to each other and talk about her behind her back, but this only serves to make her stronger and "want to *help* you more."

Honestly, she sounded like an abusive parent who tells the child, "I'm doing this for your own good," or "You made me do it." This is not the appropriate response when you act out. Making excuses for your bad acts will build resentment and preclude any possibility of a good relationship.

Apologizing makes all the difference

It's a veritable certainty there will be occasions that you and I behave badly. And when we do, we need to have the humility to recognize our wrongdoing and be quick with an apology. Often the longer we wait to apologize, the harder it gets to do so.

Fellow lawyer @frozensooner shared this story on Twitter:

> Two days ago, had a phone call with [opposing counsel] that didn't go like he'd expected. I didn't agree with him on his interpretation of the contract, and I didn't agree with his characterization of my client's actions. He got fairly heated, and when I said, "It was nice talking to you," he responded "I wish I could say the same."
>
> This is someone who's a junior partner at a fairly large firm. Not Latham, but definitely at least a major player in several states. I was taken somewhat aback.
>
> Ten minutes later, he emailed an apology.
>
> Honestly, that's all it took. I appreciated that he did that. We all get hot under the collar and say things we regret. An apology isn't necessarily as good as just not doing it, but it gives a look at your character. It takes a big person to apologize sometimes.

What makes for a good apology?

Let's start with what does not make for a good apology: "I'm sorry if you were offended by what I said." This is not an apology. It is nothing. Actually, it's not nothing, because it's likely to fuel the fire you kindled when you acted like a jerk, rather than squelch it.

A good apology has two components: contrition and specificity. When you apologize for bad behavior, you should address specifically what you said or did wrong. And your apology should reflect remorse for your deeds.

We all exhibit bad behavior sometimes. It's just going to happen. But the next time you offend opposing counsel or your assistant or your spouse, be quick to recognize your misstep and apologize.

42

EVERYBODY'S GOT A SIDE HUSTLE, BUT SHOULD LAWYERS? (PART 1)

W e live in what has been called the "gig economy." It seems like everyone has a side hustle where they're earning extra income - Uber drivers, dog walkers, ghost writers, podcasters, renting out their primary residence. You name it and there's likely a niche market. But should lawyers be looking to capitalize on this still-new and pliable economy?

Based on my law blog and book writing having been side hustles for me for a couple of years now, you should be able to anticipate my answer. If you have an interest that you can monetize, whether it complements your practice or is something apart from your work as a lawyer, you should consider engaging the endeavor. I've talked to many lawyers who have found additional fulfillment and purpose in their side hustles, which enabled them to pursue interests their daily law practices didn't touch on.

To further discuss lawyers having a side hustle, I reached out to a Tennessee lawyer, Curt Runger, who launched an attorney mentoring project a few years ago. Here's what Runger has to say about his experience.

JWR: What is your side hustle?

CR: I run AttorneyMentors.com which is a membership website where solo lawyers can go to receive training on all things related to their practice, including online and offline marketing strategies, establishing systems for their practice, practice management skills, etc. The individuals who come through my signature program, the Solo Practice Master Class, get access to over 20 hours of video training, access to a private Facebook group, regular group coaching calls and individual coaching calls with me over Zoom.

JWR: What was your motivation for starting your side hustle?

CR: I had been practicing law for 12 years and had grown my practice from a one man outfit to a team of 4 attorneys, but I really felt as though I needed a new challenge. I loved motivating people and loved marketing and wanted to incorporate those passions into a business outside my law practice. I also saw a shift in the landscape of the legal profession coming on and realized there were so many young attorneys out there who were not as lucky as I had been when it came to having a strong attorney mentor. I could see newer and younger attorneys really struggling in their practices and wanted to serve them. The best way for me to serve them was by creating AttorneyMentors.com and structuring a program that could reach people all throughout the United States.

JWR: How specifically are you able to mentor other lawyers through your program?

CR: The lawyers who come through my Solo Practice Master Class obtain mentoring in multiple ways. For starters, each lawyer begins the program with a 45 minute introductory video conference call with me, so that I can learn about their personality, their family, their core values, their practice/market, their mindset and so that I can ascertain the challenges they are facing in their law practices. After the call, I really dive deeply into their market and undertake my own independent research of them, so that I can most effectively serve them.

Additionally, the attorneys have access to a back-office on my website containing over 20 hours of video trainings which are condensed into micro segments (20 minutes or less) designed to mentor them in all aspects of their law practice from developing the proper mindset to in depth online and off-line marketing strategies and practice management skills. The videos are essentially a home-study program which enable the lawyers to go through the trainings at their own pace.

That said, the most valuable mentoring from the program comes from regular group coaching calls, as well as individual coaching calls, conducted over video conferencing. These calls give the lawyers in my program a chance to ask me specific questions about their practices in a setting that is "judgment free." I'm able to effectively mentor the attorneys in these calls because by this point, I've done my homework on them, have sized them up individually and most importantly, have researched their market. The calls are designed to help the attorneys develop strategies to improve their law practices and make more money, but also to hold them accountable with the action they must take to ensure success.

An added benefit of the group calls is that these calls are recorded and housed in the back office on my website, so everyone in my program can re-listen to the calls at any time (even if they are not on the call) and often times, I'll have clients tell me that they learned a lot simply from listening to other attorneys' questions and my answers on the calls.

JWR: Was Attorney Mentors your first entrepreneurial venture outside having a practice?

CR: Yes, and it was terrifying and totally different from starting and scaling my law practice! The crazy thing is that until I founded Attorney Mentors, I never even really considered myself an entrepreneur, despite the fact that I started a solo law practice which has now grown to five attorneys.

JWR: What was your goal for your side hustle when you started?

CR: I had multiple goals. I obviously wanted to create a business and brand that would allow me to serve solo lawyers, but I also wanted to be able to feel passionate about the work I was doing on a daily basis, something not happening practicing law. The immediate goal was to get a program together like the Solo Practice Master Class that I could be proud of and start building up Attorney Mentors brand.

JWR: What are your goals now?

CR: To really focus on the brand awareness aspect of Attorney Mentors and continue to serve solo lawyers but to do it on a much bigger scale and to expand into other areas whether it be different type continuity programs or even CLEs.

JWR: Has your side hustle been worth the effort?

CR: Absolutely. Not only do I have the satisfaction of seeing something through that I started, but the satisfaction of knowing that what I created is awesome and helps attorneys. The most satisfying thing of it too is that many of my clients in Attorney Mentors have been practicing law for 10, 15 years, and to be able to help them take their practices where they want to go is amazing.

JWR: Has Attorney Mentors had any direct effect on your practice or you as a lawyer?

CR: It's had a profound impact on my practice, and I've definitely become a better lawyer through creating the master class and working with attorneys from literally all over the United States. It helps keep me more accountable not only to my clients, but also to my associate attorneys and staff. My law firm is more efficient and more profitable because of it.

It sounds so corny, but it truly is one of those situations when I actually learn a lot just from mentoring other attorneys. I've learned so much about myself and my practice through mentoring attorneys, and I also learn valuable lessons from the lawyers who come through the program just from hearing about their experiences. In a sense, creating the program was probably the best investment that I could personally make in my law firm. What I love most about the program is that it provides an incredible learning platform for not only the lawyers who I mentor, but also myself. Just brainstorming and master-minding with attorneys can be so powerful. I love it and it has been the most rewarding experience of my professional life.

JWR: What advice would I have for others who are considering a side hustle?

CR: I could talk for an hour on this subject easily. I would say that the most important thing is that your side hustle has to be something you love. It takes an insane amount of work and you have to be willing to make major, major sacrifices sometimes to the detriment of your law practice and personal life in general. You really have to do a good job mapping out your time because your law practice clients deserve your best efforts as well, and they are the ones who are ultimately "financing" your side hustle because it takes money to build up a business.

You have to be smart about outsourcing and get good people in place for those tasks that can be outsourced. In my case, I was entering into a whole new world online. I had no clue about running a direct sales marketing business and there was a lot of stuff involved that was and that remains over my head. That being said, I was fortunate to find great people to work with and really figured out pretty quickly where my time and energy was best spent in building up my company.

The one thing you have to realize that I can't emphasize enough is that you have to be consistent and show up for your business on a daily basis. It seems so elementary, but most people who start side hustles don't ever see them through because of the massive amount of work it takes and the lack of seeing instantaneous results. You also need a proper mindset and be able to not worry about what everyone else is doing, and you have to learn to avoid self-sabotaging thoughts or habits that will hold you back if you aren't equipped to deal with them.

Do you have a side hustle that you're considering? There are plenty of examples of other lawyers who have successfully explored theirs. I can name more than a dozen right off the top of my head. Some have even been so successful with their side projects that it became their primary occupation. I recommend that you do the research to determine whether there's a market for your endeavor, then make a plan and set some goals. Or you can do what I did and just jump in more or less blindly and figure things out as you go along.

43

EVERYBODY'S GOT A SIDE HUSTLE, BUT SHOULD LAWYERS? (PART 2)

Financial Panther is a lawyer-turned-entrepreneur who, as best I can tell, is the living embodiment of the sharing economy. I wanted to interview him to share with you that you don't have to be an author or be in direct sales to have a slide hustle. You can use resources that are near at hand and start making money immediately by taking advantage of the sharing economy that has developed within the last few years.

JWR: What do you do as a side hustle?

FP: I have a lot of side hustles, but the short answer is that most of my side hustles involve the sharing economy and gig economy. Over the past several years, I've done a ton of different side hustles in the sharing/gig economy, and in any given month, I'll bring in income from 10 to 15 different sources.

Some of my side hustles include renting out a room in my house on Airbnb, dog-sitting and walking dogs with Rover and Wag, delivering food on my bike with Postmates, DoorDash, and Uber Eats, charging electric scooters with Bird and Lime, doing random tasks for people with apps like TaskRabbit, and various other side hustles in the sharing/gig economy. If you name any app that uses on-demand independent contractors, chances are I've tried it out.

JWR: What does the term "gig economy" mean to you and how have you turned it to your advantage?

FP: I think of the gig economy as including all of the different apps that you can simply turn on anytime you want and start working and earning money right away. These include all of the different apps that have really only been possible in the last few years with the rise of smartphones — think rideshare apps, food delivery apps, and dog walking apps, to name a few.

There are a lot of advantages with side hustling using gig economy apps. First, they are low risk and require basically no capital to get started. What this means is that you can try out different things. If something doesn't work out, you're really only out the time you spent on it. Second, unlike a lot of side hustles that require a ramp-up period, gig economy apps allow you to start earning income pretty much immediately. All you have to do is turn on whichever app you want to use, and get started working.

Finally, and perhaps most importantly, gig economy apps are extremely flexible, which means that it is possible to incorporate a lot of these gig economy side hustles into your day-to-day life. With limited time on your hands, being able to incorporate different gigs into the spare hours in your day is super important. With some strategic thinking, it is possible to essentially get paid for the things you're already doing anyway.

For example, I enjoy biking and do it regularly. By delivering food on my bike with apps like Postmates, DoorDash, and Uber Eats, I'm essentially able to pay myself for the time I'd already spend biking. It's like I'm getting paid to exercise.

JWR: What was your motivation for starting your side hustles?

FP: A lot of my motivation for side hustling was to find an outlet for the stress I had from my day job. When I started side hustling, I was working really long hours at a big law firm. I started these simple side hustles because I found them fun. After a lot of stressful hours in the office, it really helped me to be able to do something completely unrelated to the law, like biking around the city delivering food.

I also had a secondary goal to just sort of humble myself. As an attorney (especially at a big law firm, like I was), it's easy to get into the mindset of thinking that you are better than everyone else or that other people are beneath you. Doing these sharing economy side hustles did a lot to help me stay grounded and humble.

JWR: What was your goal for your side hustles when you started?

FP: My main goal for my various side hustles was just to try them out and see whether they were worth the effort. Once I knew how they worked, I kept doing them and saved all of the extra income I made. My rationale was that, since I was living perfectly fine on my day job income, I could save 100% of my side hustle income and dramatically increase my savings rate.

JWR: What are your goals for it now and what are your long-term plans?

FP: My current goals are to use these side hustles to basically support myself while I work on a few entrepreneurial ventures in the coming year. One of the great things with these side hustles is that they provide a pretty nice floor for me - I don't need a ton of money, and I pretty much know I can use my side hustles to cover the bills while I continue to work on my blog and other projects.

JWR: Has your side hustle been worth the effort?

FP: I'd say that absolutely, all of my side hustles have been worth the effort. They're fun, which is the most important thing. And honestly, they don't really feel like much work to me since most of my side hustles have pretty much been incorporated into my day-to-day life.

JWR: What advice would you have for others who are considering a side hustle?

FP: Don't be afraid to try things that are totally unrelated to your legal training. There are a lot of people out there who think that side hustles need to be something that builds on what you do in your day job. That may work for someone who really loves what they're doing all day, but I suspect that a lot of people are looking for side hustles, not just to make extra income, but also to follow different passions. If you have something you're interested in, don't be afraid to give it a try.

What I've learned from Financial Panther is to have the boldness to explore new low-cost opportunities. They may not work out, and if that's so, you'll have lost only the time it took to have a new adventure of sorts. His exploits into the sharing economy have given him the financial freedom to make career decisions that suit him and have helped keep him from being bound to a job due to a lack of other income streams. If you're looking for some financial independence or methods of relieving stress, participating in the sharing economy as a side hustle may be the cure for what ails you.

44

PURSUING YOUR PASSION PROJECTS

I t isn't often that a novel can hurtle you decades into your own past and rekindle thoughts of people and feelings long since buried in the hubris of life. For me *The Barrowfields* was such a book. Readers meet book's protagonist Henry as an adolescent North Carolina boy and journey with him into adulthood, through both adventures and tragedy. When Henry went to law school and his experience was more-or-less appropriately harrowing, I looked to see if the author of *The Barrowfields*, Phillip Lewis, was a lawyer by trade. When I discovered that he is a lawyer with a practice in North Carolina, I decided to reach out to him.

Many of us desire to engage in endeavors other than, or (perhaps more appropriately) in addition to, the practice of law, whether it's passion projects or side hustles. But so few actually do it. There are many obligations and driving factors that allow us to be deterred. Phillip Lewis had a dream, and he was not dissuaded from pursuing it.

Here's my interview with Phillip Lewis about making the decision to follow his dreams and taking the steps necessary to achieve them.

JWR: When did you know that you wanted to write a novel?

PL: I grew up in a small town in the mountains of North Carolina called West Jefferson, in Ashe County, which is stuck right up there in the northwestern corner of the state next to Tennessee and Virginia. It was, and still is, a very beautiful place, but I recall it from my youth also as a place where you could look for and easily find all manner of human conditions, from severe poverty, to new-found, yet meager, wealth (old family money was almost nonexistent); people living, often resolutely, with disease and disability; people living and coping with loss, and finding joy and hope in small places.

You'd drive around and on the main highway there'd be a man sitting in his front yard, right in front of his house, a white T-shirt on, eyeglasses too large for his face, just watching the traffic go by for hours on end and probably remembering a time from long before when it was a two-lane road instead of a four-lane. In a field running up a hillside there were muddy black cows, and in the next pasture over, an old mare with a bowed spine and her ribs showing, and a timeless old creek coming down out of the hills.

Down the street: men standing at the gas station, talking, some of them in overalls. Spit on the ground. Cowboy boots; work boots. Up behind the town, at the municipal park, a little-league baseball game in the 6th inning with everyone in town interested in the outcome and looking forward to reading about it in the next day's paper. And then in the early evening a funeral procession on Highway 194 to the family cemetery, way up on top of the hill, and *every* car coming the other way stops and turns its lights on to show respect as the procession passes. Every single one of them, the people, profound in their simplicity, resilient in their determination to live each day, and the next one after that, assured by simple truths and spiritualisms and practical aphorisms that contain multitudes of truth. You can't paint everyone with the same brush, of course, but this was what you'd see before you looked any closer.

By the time I graduated from high school, I'd concluded that this world in the mountains was, at its honest core, a place imbued with a fundamental sadness, and also with a deep sincerity of living that may not exist anywhere else. It was a place that longed for a fair description. And it is where I experienced, time and again, a deep sense of quiet melancholy, of simple human tragedies, that I longed, and still long, to describe. From as early as I can remember, I wanted to paint these landscapes and draw these portraits.

JWR: Having some experience with this myself — there is a difference between wanting to write and actually doing the work of writing. When did you decide to write your novel?

PL: I started writing *The Barrowfields* in earnest about seven years ago, but I do not remember a specific moment in time when I thought, "I'm going to do this. I'm going to write a novel."

Starting off writing your first novel is a bit like contemplating the construction of an Egyptian pyramid or building a rocket intended for space travel. You have no idea at the outset whether what you are about to attempt is possible; whether you have the ability or the wherewithal to complete the task; or whether you're going to die trying before you reach the end. Psychologically, it's easier if you fool yourself into thinking that you're not at the beginning of a years-long journey that will eventually consume you entirely and take a magnificent toll on your family and everyone around you, but instead that you're just putting up the framing for what will eventually be a small house, but which you know in the back of your mind will almost certainly evolve into a hillside mansion.

All of this is just to say that I had no Eureka moment, no decisive morning on which I arose and declared my intention of writing a novel. It just began, and as it grew older, it sprouted legs and grew until it finally achieved the form it has today.

JWR: I've heard tell that when he was a practicing lawyer, John Grisham set aside time every morning to write before beginning his billable work. How did you create time to write?

PL: I met John recently and the very first thing he said to me was that, as a writer, you have to have rigid discipline that includes setting aside time to write every day. I think he still follows this routine, and obviously it has worked well when you consider that he's now published more than 25 books and he's still going.

My writing schedule for *The Barrowfields*, with first one young child at home, and then two before the book was finished, did not allow for anything approaching regularity, but I nevertheless found myself working on the book at every spare moment of the day. I'd often get up and write in the mornings while everyone else in the house was still sleeping. For me, this writing time was the best and the most lucid, but it was also the shortest.

I would often write for a few hours once I got to work, before I was overwhelmed with client emails and telephone calls and appellate deadlines and the like. On days when I had court, I'd get to the courthouse early and write before my hearings started. Anyone who knows me well knows that a lot of my CLE time was spent writing and working on *The Barrowfields*.

At night after work, I would resume writing once the children were in bed—a few ounces of good bourbon at the ready—and this time was good for reviewing the day's writing and reading it aloud to myself to gauge for tempo and rhythm and meter. Wherever I went I had a notebook with me, and usually a laptop computer, so that if I found myself with any amount of time, I would set to work on the book. At the bar in Poe's Tavern in Charleston was a favorite place of mine to write.

JWR: Were your partners aware that you were planning to write a novel? And if so, were they supportive of your endeavor?

PL: My partners gradually learned of my work on a novel as it progressed, and they were more supportive than you can imagine. I'm still amazed by this. It was routine for other lawyers in the firm to come by and ask how the book was progressing and have a real interest in it.

Several of them read and commented on drafts along the way. At each milestone—when I found an agent; when we first sold the publishing rights; when the first galleys came in, etc.—they celebrated with me and helped spread the good news. During periods of time for which my work on the book significantly cut into my lawyer time, the other lawyers in my litigation group took over cases for me, handled my hearings, wrote my briefs, and in general made it possible for me to focus almost entirely on the book.

I honestly don't know if there's another law firm anywhere that would have been as supportive, and I couldn't have done it without all that help.

JWR: In what ways has your being an author affected your practice?

PL: Being an author has had an enormous impact on my practice. I feel very much like I've had two full-time jobs for the past few years, but only one of them pays with regularity.

I've spent countless days away from the office visiting bookstores or speaking to organizations or book clubs since *The Barrowfields* came out in March 2017. Before then, in the final two years before publication, I missed out on *a lot* of billable hours because I was busy writing and editing. Even now, more than a year after publication, there are frequent opportunities to focus on book-related matters.

For example, a German translation of *The Barrowfields* is in the works, and the translator in Berlin is wonderfully detailed and precise. She has contacted me many times to discuss language and implication found in *The Barrowfields*, and how that may be successfully communicated in German, which has been more challenging than I anticipated.

So it seems that there is always something book-related which has a way of taking my attention away from practicing law. My hope is that all the marketing effort on behalf of the book will eventually bring some good new business for the firm, because I certainly feel I owe them that after the kindness and patience they have shown to me. I'm starting to see this more and more, and I hope it will continue.

JWR: What advice would you give to other lawyers who want to pursue a passion project or side hustle?

PL: First, you just have to decide to do it. If you wait until "the time is right," it will likely never happen. Second, if you are writing a book, understand that it's damn hard work, but it's supposed to be.

People get frustrated when they sit down to write and run into the first of what will be a series of walls that are hard to see around. You just have to know going in that it's a slog, and that's the reality of it. If you're like most writers, there's no such thing as instant gratification. Read *The Autobiography of an American Novelist* by Thomas Wolfe and you'll see you're not alone in this.

Third, you have to be willing to believe in yourself despite clear and convincing evidence to the contrary. Along the way, you will be beset by innumerable distractions and naysayers, and you'll be presented time and again with plenty of reason to believe that what you're attempting is a fool's errand.

You have to firmly decide "to hell with all that," and just keep working, even though there's part of you that thinks the naysayers could be right.

I have hobbies and interests that take away from time I could otherwise be working and billing clients. This book for example, my law blog, running and fly fishing (which I wrote about in *Building a Better Law Practice*). It took me years to come to terms with it being okay to take time for myself. But now I understand that having a hobby and taking time to recharge are essential, not only for a healthy me, but also for a healthier practice. Although times are a-changin' that's still a minority view in many circles.

If you are a lawyer considering or in the midst of pursuing a side hustle or passion project, allow this interview to offer reinforcement or encouragement you may need to hear.

45

SEEK THE MISSION THAT GIVES YOUR
LIFE MEANING

I n *Man's Search for Meaning*, Viktor E. Frankl writes," One
should not search for an abstract meaning of life.
Everyone has his own specific vocation or mission in life
to carry out a concrete assignment which demands fulfillment."
We are daily bombarded with so much attention and focus
on being superficially *happy*, but I believe this is a misguided
notion. Happiness is neither a means nor an end. It is a
byproduct of a life lived with meaning and purpose. Happiness
is not a thing to be chased for its own sake. It is too fleeting and
circumstantial to be the goal that our actions strive to achieve.
In seeking happiness, you will find yourself like the raccoon
who flits from one shiny object to the next. Rather, we should
pursue things of greater substance. The accomplishment of
these greater purposes may yield happiness as a result.

Two of the things that provide purpose for me are my faith
and family. I want to be a good steward of the gifts that have
been bestowed upon me, and I want to be a good provider for
my family. Aside from my profession as a lawyer, my writing is
one of the tangible ways I tend to those purposes. But there are
other internal and external motivators for my writing as well.

Following my interview with Phillip Lewis, he turned the tables and asked me where does the drive come from to write the blog and my book, *Building a Better Law Practice*. I likely gave him much more answer than he was seeking, but here's how I responded:

> Well, I try to be pretty self-aware, so I know there are many layers to that answer. Since I was a teenager, writing has been very important to me, although then it was creative writing. I wrote a lot of poetry over the course of 10 or 12 years.
>
> When I was working on my master's in history (I taught high school before going to law school), I wrote a couple of papers that got published in historical journals. Then once I went to law school and started practicing, all the extracurricular writing stopped for a couple of years. I just had a hard time justifying doing it when there was billable work to be done.
>
> But in 2016 (my fourth year of practice), I realized that to build my own insurance defense practice, I would have do something outside the box. So I started my law blog. I wandered in the wilderness of obscurity with few readers for 6 or 8 months, before things started to get a little traction. About that same time, I started branching out from the appellate case summaries I had been writing to writing about other topics.
>
> And I discovered I am interested in and have a lot to say about managing clients, cases, and a practice. So those topics have been the bulk of my writing now for the last 16 months or so.
>
> As we get to the less healthy end of the answer to your question - I'm a 3 on the Enneagram (an achiever/performer), so whether I prefer it or not, it's important to me what my peers think of me and the things I'm accomplishing. The blog

and now the book have been a way to set myself apart from the crowd.

I'm also motivated to pay off my substantial student loans, so I hope these things can help get me there.

That's probably more than you were asking for, but those are certainly the motivators I've identified.

That is a bit more personal than I normally get in my writing, but it's so important that we find a sense of meaning and purpose about our work that I felt compelled to share it. I was listening to Jeff Goins's interview with Shawn Askinosie on *The Portfolio Life*, and Askinosie made this statement: "If we can find some meaning in our lives, we're going to live longer, be more joyful, and be more pleasant to be around."[1] Askinosie is a former litigator who decided to get out of the business of law and started a chocolate company.

Maybe your sense of meaning isn't tied to your vocation. Perhaps your vocation is the vehicle that enables you to do the other things that give you purpose. Whatever the case, once you've found that purpose, don't lose sight of it. It will help you stay grounded and motivated. Working with purpose can help you avoid the burnout that afflicts too many who are working furiously but with no clear direction.

46

THE IMPORTANCE OF SETTING GOALS

G ood goals are a beacon to let you know you are headed in the right direction. They enable you throughout the course of a year to review your list to affirm whether you are taking actions to help you achieve the goals you have set.

Without goals, you are a boat adrift at sea. You can paddle as hard as you're able, for as long as you can, in whatever direction you see fit. But without a specific destination in mind and a beacon to guide you, there is no correct direction for you to travel. Your efforts become flitting and circular.

More often though, if you do not set your own goals, someone else will impose his goals on you. Your efforts then will be achieving someone else's agenda. Not growing your own business. Not building your own practice. Not seeking what is in your own best interest. Instead, you will be a cog in another's machine. And that is the best case scenario.

The other alternative is that you go nowhere at all. A body at rest tends to stay at rest unless some other force acts on it. Without goals to guide you, you may just sit in stagnant doldrums toiling away, accomplishing nothing.

Setting Goals Has Real Effects

I started setting goals three years ago. Now, when the leaves start to turn, my mind also turns to ruminating on the upcoming year and what I want to accomplish in the next 12 month cycle. I will start scribbling things down, and eventually, I will formalize a list as the calendar rolls into December. This method has served me well. It enables me to know what actions I need to take throughout the year to accomplish what I have set out to do.

There is a system I like to use for setting goals: S.M.A.R.T. goals are Specific, Measurable, Achievable, Results-focused, and Time-bound. The University of Virginia provides the following helpful definitions[1]:

- **Specific:** Goals should be written simply and define what you intend to do.
- **Measurable:** Goals should be measurable so that you have tangible evidence that you have accomplished the goal. Usually, the entire goal statement is a measure for a project, but there are often short-term objectives built into the goal.
- **Achievable:** Goals should be achievable; they should stretch you so you feel challenged, but be defined well enough so you can achieve them. You must have or develop the appropriate knowledge, skills, and abilities needed to achieve the goals.
- **Results-focused:** Goals should measure outcomes, not activities.
- **Time-bound:** Goals should be linked to a timeframe that creates a sense of urgency, or results in tension between the current reality and the vision of the goal. Without such tension, the goal is unlikely to produce a relevant outcome.

You May Not Achieve All Your Goals

Most recently, in 2018, I did not accomplish all the goals I set for myself, but I moved the ball forward. I am in a better position in 2019 to reset and achieve those goals, than if I had never set them.

There are other goals I have accomplished. In 2017, I set out to publish my first book the following year. I signed a book contract in late November 2017, but there was still a long row to hoe before the book could enter the world. Lots of writing and rewriting (and more rewriting). Working with the good folks at the ABA. Then in June 2018, days before my daughter was born, my book *Building a Better Law Practice* was sitting on bookshelves.

Setting Goals for Your Law Practice

As it related to my practice goals for 2018, I wanted to strengthen and develop my relationships with a few specific clients. Keeping that in mind helped me do things throughout the year that would continue to build our business relationship through trust and collaborative processes.

To help you keep your goals in mind, I recommend you put them somewhere they are visible to you. A constant reminder to take affirmative steps and make strategic decisions toward achieving them. I have seen people frame their list of goals and hang it on the wall. Others have made them the backgrounds on phones and monitors.

However you choose to do it, if you are not already setting personal or professional goals for yourself, now is the time to start. Setting goals is your opportunity to take control of your future and work toward the practice you want for yourself, rather than the future someone else will impose on you if you do not fill that void yourself.

47

FACTORS THAT CONTRIBUTE TO YOUR SUCCESS

Y ou have ultimate control over your own success or failure. The locus of control is squarely within your domain. It's important that you understand that. This isn't to say everything you attempt will succeed no matter how badly you want it — certainly it will not. But there are things you can control to determine your ultimate success. Here are three factors that contribute to your success.

1. Talent

You have no control over whether you have talent in a particular area. Or even the amount of talent you do or do not have. Talent is a genetic gift bestowed on each of us in different ways, giving us the capacity to do certain things better than others. But since you can't control it, forget about it.

Steph Curry wasn't born as one of the greatest shooters of his or any other generation. He's undersized and has bad ankles. He didn't attend one of the basketball blueblood schools. Even in his first couple of years in the NBA, Curry was solid but did not evidence an ability to rise to one of the best couple of players in the NBA. He lacked the natural talent that oozes out of guys like Lebron James. But Curry didn't resolve himself to being a good player. He sought out greatness. He worked tirelessly, daily, year after year. He honed his craft until his greatness was apparent to everyone.

If you want to achieve a skill or master a craft, do it regardless of talent. The guy with more talent than you may start with a leg up, but he doesn't monopolize whatever space you want to occupy.

I am not the most gifted litigator. Plenty of people are inherently better orators than me. There are any number of better writers than me. But that knowledge does not give me permission to resolve myself to being a second-rate lawyer. It arms me with resolution to work harder and to become better.

If you want to achieve greatness, do it regardless of talent. Make talent inconsequential by being willing to put in the work.

2. Luck

You know what else is beyond your control? Luck. Whether good luck or bad. You can't count on it, and you shouldn't despair over it.

Sometimes you will have bad luck. You might be like me and buy your first house in 2007 at peak market prices right before the biggest economic decline since the Great Depression. Then you're stuck with it for years before eventually taking a huge loss on it. That's just bad luck. And sometimes there's just not really anything to learn from those situations.

Or you might be like author Elizabeth Gilbert. She's written seven books. One of them was a worldwide bestseller for more than two years - *Eat, Pray, Love*. None of her other books have seen the same economic success. Was that one book so much better than her others? Probably not. It was the right book at the right time, and it struck a chord with millions of readers. That is luck.

You can't count on luck. But you can and must pursue your work so that when luck turns its eye your way, you can benefit from it. Coleman Cox is attributed with writing, "I'm a great believer in luck. The harder I work, the more of it I seem to have." Discount luck. Just do your work.

3. Work Ethic

You see where this is going. You may not be as gifted as someone else, or be handed the same opportunities. But you can let your drive and ambition guide you to outwork others. I'm not necessarily advocating that you work 60 hours a week, but that might be necessary. I'm certainly not suggesting you sacrifice time with your family or forego your health.

What I'm telling you is you need to work more efficiently and effectively than others in your space. But really, don't pay them any mind. Put your head down and your blinders on. Do the work you need to do. Have goals so you know where you're headed. Then do your work. Give no thought to talent or luck or any number of other things that you cannot control. Concern yourself only with what is at your fingertips. Be diligent and tenacious in achieving.

Now close this book and get to work.

48

CHARACTER TRAITS, NOT SKILLS

BONUS CHAPTER FOR NEW LAWYERS

W hen interviewing job candidates, law firms are generally interested not in the particular skills that you've acquired at law school, clerkships, or over your career, but in your inherent personal qualities. No one reasonably expects you to come out of law school knowing how to practice law, take an effective deposition, or draft a motion for summary judgment. Typically, it makes no difference if your other hands-on experience was in the areas of practice the firm or your anticipated practice group is dealing with daily. Firms can teach those things. What firms are most concerned with are your character traits, your work ethic, your natural inclinations. Here are some areas that firms are looking for in clerks or associate candidates.

Are You Teachable?

You and I know plenty of people who believe they're the smartest person to occupy any given room. Those folks often cannot take instruction, unwilling to learn new methods, and unable to adapt or be malleable. They will have a tough time growing and becoming the best lawyers they otherwise could be.

Teachability is one of the most important aspects of succeeding. It involves balancing pride and humility. You need to have a pride about yourself that motivates you to want to improve your craft, and the humility to be able to internalize and implement criticism and instruction. Nothing will turn off a firm's interest in a candidate quicker than perceiving they are aloof to criticism or a have propensity for disregarding suggestions.

You are entering a profession in which a "practice" is a continuous evolution of accumulated knowledge and applied wisdom. You cannot afford to walk in the door with more ego than introspection.

Do You Play Well with Others?

A few years ago, a friend's firm hired a new associate. Within the first couple of weeks, my friend, his partner, and the new associate were standing around trying to decide what to do about lunch. No one wanted to drive, so my friend joked with the new guy that since he was lowest on the totem pole, he'd be driving. He lost his head! He bowed up, yelling that he wasn't going to be picked on like that and no one should be treated the way my friend had treated him. My friend thought he was about to get punched. You don't want to be the guy who doesn't get along with his coworkers and loses control of himself.

Most of us practice in small legal markets. We will be working with and against the same people for forty years. There are plenty of lawyers who are inclined to make every case personal and want to fight about everything and just generally make the lives of the people around them difficult. Some act this way because they think it's the best avenue for getting their way and others because it's the precedent that was set for them by older lawyers. But it does nothing to establish good will or functional working relationships.

Your reputation will be established early in your career. And if that reputation is one of being difficult and unreasonable, it is a reputation that's going to be tough to shed. Firms are looking for lawyers who know how to collaborate with others and communicate effectively (which isn't to say there aren't times when being ornery is necessary and proper).

Are You Willing to Put in the Hours (and Not Just the Billable Ones)?

During law school, I clerked with a district attorney's office, a municipal judge, a couple of civil solo practitioners, and a real estate attorney. I had no experience in trucking defense litigation, which is where I spent most of my first four years of practice. I had virtually no knowledge of the insurance and trucking industries, and certainly no familiarity with the regulations governing them. And I had no expectation that over the course of the next five years, I would peruse hundreds of thousands of pages of medical records.

You are likely going to enter a field with which you are largely unfamiliar. That is to be expected. You will need to be a quick study. Depending on the firm that hires you, your billable hour requirements may be hefty. But there's going to be knowledge you must acquire that you're going to be unable to bill to obtain. It will require perseverance and dedication to develop the base of knowledge necessary to be proficient in your practice area. Your interviewer is looking for cues that you are not only willing to meet your billable requirements but also put in that extra time it takes to develop your craft and become a truly good lawyer.

How Can You Exhibit These Qualities in an Interview?

Just be you. The firm will know whether you have the qualities they are looking for. If, on the other hand, you are in a blind interview, you have about an hour to impress upon your interviewers that you have the characteristics they are look for in a candidate. The personalities of the people who are interviewing you and types of questions being asked will be indications of whether you're a good fit for each other, as will the firm's reputation among other lawyers. Remember, the interview is a two-way street. As much as they are sizing you up, you ought to be doing the same with them, because the firm's reputation and perceived qualities will become yours, just as soon as you're associated with it.

NOTES

4. Litigation Budgets Should Reflect Reality

1. Association of Corporate Counsel, "How to Prepare a Litigation Plan and Budget," www.accmeetings.com.

8. Law Firm Marketing Myths: Marketing Is for Extroverts

1. Cain, Susan, *Quiet: The Power of Introverts in a World That Can't Stop Talking*, p. 11 (Kindle Edition), Crown/Archetype.
2. Cain, p. 264 (Kindle Edition).

11. Where Law Firm Websites Go Wrong and How to Fix It

1. Miller, Donald. *Building a StoryBrand: Clarify Your Message So Customers Will Listen,* Loc. 352, HarperCollins Leadership (Kindle Edition).
2. Miller, Loc. 2204 (Kindle Edition).
3. Miller, Loc. 2032 (Kindle Edition).

14. Frame Your Daily Tasks in a More Productive Light

1. A version of this article first appeared in the "Your Voice" feature of the *ABA Journal*.

22. Should You Ask Judges If They Are Familiar with Your Case?

1. A version of this article first appeared in the "Your Voice" feature of the *ABA Journal*.

26. Have Something to Say but Not Sure You're Qualified?

1. A version of this article first appeared in the "Your Voice" feature of the *ABA Journal*.

27. What Do Associates Want from Their Firms?

1. A version of this article first appeared in the "Your Voice" feature of the *ABA Journal*.
2. U.S. Office of Personnel Management, "Performance Management: Performance Cycle Management," www.opm.gov.

40. Being Smart Isn't as Impressive as You Think

1. A version of this article first appeared in the "Your Voice" feature of the *ABA Journal*.

45. Seek the Mission That Gives Your Life Meaning

1. *The Portfolio Life* Podcast with Jeff Goins, May 17, 2018.

46. The Importance of Setting Goals

1. University of Virginia HR, "Writing SMART Goals" [accessed October 2018].

ALSO BY JEREMY W. RICHTER

Building a Better Law Practice: Become a Better Lawyer in Five
Minutes a Day

ACKNOWLEDGMENTS

This book would not have been possible without the contributions of the dozens of lawyers, particularly in the LawyerSmack community and on Twitter, who participated in interviews and with whom I had countless conversations, the subjects of which became the content of this book.

My wife and kids have been endlessly patient as I worked on the book on the weekends. Or at least, my wife has been endlessly patient. My 4-year-old has tolerated it, though his tolerance has been interjected with regular inquiries about when we can play. And the infant is mostly indifferent about it.

Special thanks goes to Keith Lee, who has actively mentored me about my law blog, books, and other pursuits over the last couple of years.

ABOUT THE AUTHOR

Jeremy W. Richter practices civil defense litigation in Birmingham, Alabama. He discovered early in his practice that managing cases is only half the battle in the practice of law. Building and maintaining relationships with clients is equally important. Jeremy has set out to innovate ways to develop client relationships and improve methods for achieving efficient and effective results. He has written both this and his first book, *Building a Better Law Practice*, to chronicle his efforts and lessons learned along the way. Jeremy also authors a law blog at www.jeremywrichter.com.